Lovebirds

Complete Care
Made Easy ™

Lovebirds

A Guide to Caring for Your Lovebird

By Nikki Moustaki

Photographs by Eric Ilasenko

BOWTIE
PRESS®

Irvine, California

Karla Austin, *Business Operations Manager*
Nick Clemente, *Special Consultant*
Barbara Kimmel, *Managing Editor*
Jarelle S. Stein, *Editor*
Jerry G. Walls, *Technical Editor*
Rose Gordon, *Consulting Editor*
Honey Winters, *Designer*
Indexed by Melody Englund

The lovebirds in this book are referred to as *he* or *she* in alternating chapters unless their gender is apparent from the activity discussed.

Photographs copyright © 2006 Eric Ilasenko. Photographs on pages 9, 46, 107, and 141 courtesy of Ellen Uittenbogaad@www.ellen-parrots.com. Photograph on page 88 © 1995 PhotoDisc, Inc.

Library of Congress Cataloging-in-Publication Data

Moustaki, Nikki, 1970-
  Lovebirds : a guide to caring for your lovebird / by Nikki Moustaki ;
  photographs by Eric Ilasenko.
     p. cm. — (Complete care made easy)
  Includes index.
  ISBN 1-931993-92-0
  1. Lovebirds. I. Title. II. Series.

  SF473.L6M68 2006
  636.6'864—dc22
          2006010505

BowTie Press®
A Division of BowTie, Inc.
3 Burroughs
Irvine, California 92618

Printed and bound in Singapore
10 9 8 7 6 5 4 3 2 1

Acknowledgments

Thanks to everyone at BowTie Press who worked on this book, especially my lovely and irrepressible editor, Jarelle Stein.

—Nikki Moustaki

Contents

1

The Splendid Lovebird

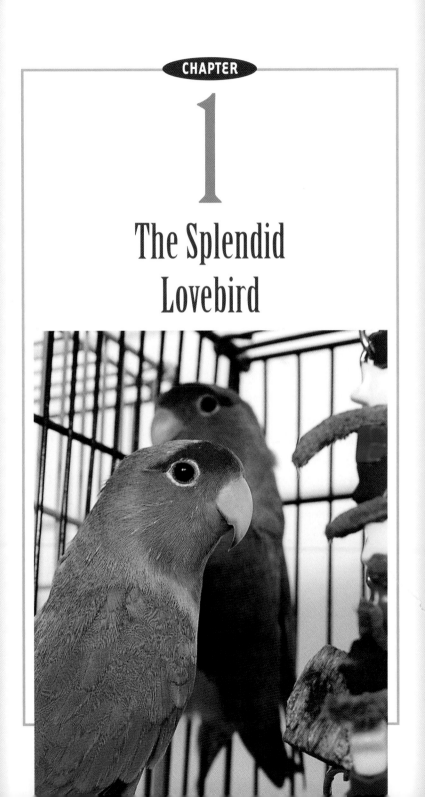

This is a pair of peach-faced lovebirds, one of the most popular species available today.

THE FRENCH CALL THESE BIRDS *LES INSÉPARABLES*—THE inseparables. Their genus name is *Agapornis*, which stems from the Greek *agape*, meaning "love," and the Greek *ornis*, meaning "bird." To the average person, they are lovebirds, a name that conjures images of affectionate birds sitting side by side on a swing, their heads together, calm and sweet. The romantic myth about lovebirds is that they will pine away and die if housed alone, and although this belief is incorrect, it shows how powerful our associations are with this small parrot. Lovebirds are wonderful pets, but they are also among the most aggressive and territorial of the commonly kept parrots. They are feisty to a fault, but they can also be incredibly sweet and loyal, making them great hands-on pets for the owner who has the patience to deal with a little bit of mischief.

What Is a Lovebird?

Lovebirds are small parrots. On average, they are about six inches long and have typical parrot features. They are acrobatic and active. The powerful beak is large in comparison with the head and is shaped like a hook (lovebirds are considered hookbills). The nostrils are barely visible in the narrow strip of naked skin at the base of the upper beak, known as the cere. Lovebirds have zygodactyl feet, which means that the feet are formed in an X shape, with two toes in front and two behind. This allows the bird to climb and hang as well as perch. Lovebirds waddle like ducks when walking on the ground instead of hopping, as other small birds do. The tail is short and bluntly rounded rather than long and tapered.

All but one species of lovebirds have large dark eyes that remain dark through adulthood. This blue black-masked lovebird also has a prominent white eye ring.

Lovebirds have large eyes that generally stay dark as the birds mature; juveniles in most parrot species are hatched with dark eyes that lighten as the birds mature. Of the nine species of lovebirds, only one, the rare *Agapornis swindernianus*, the black-collared lovebird, has a light eye—bright yellow—in the adult. Unlike other parrots, eye color can't be used to help determine the age of a lovebird. However, immature birds typically have black lines and smudges on the beak for about three months, and their plumage colors are subdued compared with the brighter plumage of adults.

Unlike budgies and cockatiels, who are the only species in their genera, there are nine species of lovebirds in the genus *Agapornis*. Many of the species in the genus can interbreed, which shows how closely they are related, in contrast to budgies, who can't successfully interbreed with any other species.

Lovebird History

The first lovebird known to Europeans was the red-faced lovebird. This bird was written about in the 1600s and was the first lovebird imported to Europe in the 1800s. The remaining eight species were discovered and imported to Europe over the next two hundred years, where they found their way into zoos and the pet trade. In particular, the peach-faced, the Fischer's, and the masked lovebirds did particularly well in captivity.

Unfortunately, the remaining six of the nine species of lovebirds never became widely established in the fancy (hobby) as breeding birds. They either need special breeding conditions or don't adapt well to caged conditions and the food being offered in captivity. Some are shy, such as the Madagascar lovebird, and don't make the best hands-on pets.

The captive-bred lovebirds we have today resulted from the importation of wild birds from Africa, with nearly all of the species entering the market in Europe and eventually the United States in the early 1900s. Tens of thousands of lovebirds were exported from Africa each year, with many of the birds failing to adapt and dying as a result of capture. Some lovebirds, such as the Abyssinian and Nyasa, weren't as abundant as the others within their very small habitats but were still prey for local trappers. In some cases, populations collapsed, and species of lovebirds went from abundant to rare in a matter of a decade or two. Today, some

Discovering Lovebirds

EUROPEAN SCIENTISTS DISCOVERED THE NINE SPECIES of lovebirds more than two hundred years ago. The following list gives the nine scientific names of the lovebirds, the person who named them, the year they were first written about, and where they were first found.

Red-faced lovebird: Agapornis pullarius Linnaeus, 1758, probably Ghana

Madagascar or grey-headed lovebird: Agapornis canus Gmelin, 1788, Madagascar and Mauritius

Abyssinian lovebird: Agapornis taranta Stanley, 1814, Ethiopia

Peach-faced lovebird: Agapornis roseicollis Vieillot, 1818, Cape Province, South Africa

Black-collared lovebird: Agapornis swindernianus Kuhl, 1820, Liberia

Black-masked lovebird: Agapornis personata Reichenow, 1887, Tanzania

Fischer's lovebird: Agapornis fischeri Reichenow, 1887, Tanzania

Nyasa lovebird: Agapornis lilianae Shelley, 1894, Malawi

Black-cheeked lovebird: Agapornis nigrigenis Sclater, 1906, Zambia

This is a young yellow black-masked lovebird; the head will darken as the bird matures.

species, such as the Abyssinian and Nyasa, are likely to be found only in protected national parks and forests.

The United States and many European countries passed restrictive laws against imported parrots in the 1970s and increased the restrictions again in the early 1990s. Today, few imported lovebirds are available legally in the United States. So there is no need to worry that buying lovebirds is harming the wild lovebird population somewhere in Africa. The lovebirds sold today were hatched and raised in captivity.

Lovebirds in the Wild

All nine lovebird species are found in mainland Africa except for one, the Madagascar lovebird (*Agapornis canus*), which is found on the large island of Madagascar off the southeastern coast of Africa. In general, lovebirds are flocking parrots of the open forests and grasslands of central Africa, extending from the western side of the continent (where they often are just isolated populations left over from when lovebirds were more generally distributed in the area) to near the Red Sea in the northeast and south to the area of the African Great Lakes (Victoria, Tanganyika, Malawi) in central Africa and to Namibia and Cape Province, South Africa, in the southwest.

A single green black-masked lovebird perches in a tree. In the wild, lovebirds tend to gather in small flocks.

Their Habitat

In the wild, lovebirds tend to spend the day in groups of five to twenty birds or more, resting and feeding in treetops. Lovebirds also feed on the ground—on grain crops and wild plants and grasses—and they can be a pest to farmers. They fly in fast spurts and are generally noisy when flying. Most mate for life but will take another mate if one is lost. In captivity, pairs also mate for life, but pairs in lovebird colonies have been known to have love affairs on the side.

Lovebirds prefer arid scrublands, savannas, and wooded grasslands close to the edges of cultivated land and never far from a reliable water source. Peach-faced lovebirds, the most commonly kept and bred species, have done very well in the wild in Arizona, where escaped pet birds have successfully created small flocks. They nest in cacti and feed on fruit and grasses, as well as in backyard bird feeders. I have seen small flocks of healthy-looking, feral peach-faced lovebirds feeding on the ground in South Florida.

Lovebirds prefer habitats near an abundant supply of water. At the edges of the African range, however, water can be scarce, and lovebirds in the southwestern and northeastern parts of Africa may be nomadic at times of the year when drought dries up nearby streams and ponds. Nomadic flocks are especially likely to feed on cultivated crops.

Some lovebirds—such as the Abyssinian lovebird—live at elevated ranges that get quite cool; these birds require a diet higher in fat than do others who live in more temperate climates. The Abyssinian and the Madagascar lovebirds also feed on wild figs, and the black-collared lovebird feeds nearly exclusively on figs.

Their Feeding Places

Lovebirds generally forage in the heads of bushes and trees, and they also come to the ground for grass seeds and planted crops, such as millet, rice, sesame, and corn. They feed in small flocks, but in some cases more than two hundred lovebirds have been seen descending on an especially fertile feeding ground. Where they have learned to raid crops, they are treated as pests and killed, although they are not nearly as destructive as many of the larger parrots.

Their Breeding Places

Although lovebirds roost (sleep and rest) communally, they break off from the flock into pairs to breed. The eye-ring lovebirds tend to nest communally, but other species are solitary and become intolerant of other birds who venture too close to where they are nesting.

Lovebirds create their nests using several different methods, depending on the species. Some find a deep tree hole (often an abandoned woodpecker or barbet hole) and line the bottom with a compact pad of leaves, bark, and grasses, as well as feathers. In most cases, it appears that the female does most of the nest-making and choosing of the site. Several species take over the large woven nests of weaver finches (which in Africa occur by the dozens in large trees) and lay their eggs there with no further preparation. Sometimes lovebirds add plant matter to existing holes in trees, crevices in cliff faces, and even holes in old buildings. The red-faced lovebirds build their nests inside arboreal termite mounds—the temperature inside the mound is warm and fairly constant, allowing the hen to leave her eggs to feed while they are incubating. (See chapter 8 for more detail on the breeding patterns of lovebirds.)

Lovebirds as Pets

Many pet shops carry three popular species of lovebirds: peach-faced (the most popular), Fischer's, and black-masked. The other species are either hard to find, rare, or unavailable. A great many lovebirds sold today are color mutations of the normal color—or nominate—bird and bear little resemblance to the wild colors of their species.

This is an orange-faced mutation of the green variety of peach-faced lovebirds.

As long as you give your feathered companion plenty of attention, she won't miss the company of another bird.

It is a common belief that lovebirds have to be kept in pairs in order to survive. This isn't the case. A single lovebird with an attentive, loving human friend is thrilled to be part of that odd couple. However, a lovebird who is going to spend a great deal of time alone with no hands-on attention from a human companion should probably have another lovebird as a friend and cage mate.

Although lovebirds are common pet birds and sell for generally moderate prices, depending on the species and the mutation, it is difficult to recommend them as pets for children or for someone not very experienced with birds. The primary reason is that they can often be quite aggressive—both to other birds and to their owners. A lovebird's beak is sharp and powerful, and this bird is not afraid to use it. However, that warning aside, lovebirds can also be incredibly loyal and sweet, wanting nothing more than to hang out with their human best friend, preening your hair and crawling inside your clothing. They are playful and active but often are content to sit on your shoulder and take a nap while you watch TV.

2

A Look at
Lovebird Species

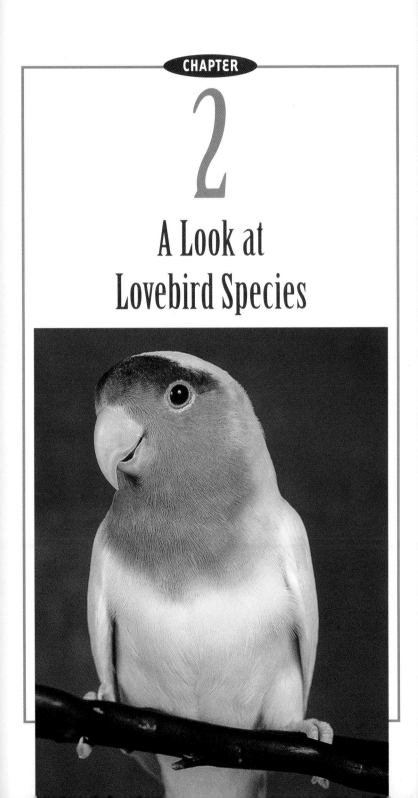

The Fischer's lovebird is one of the three most common species of pet lovebirds. This is an unusual blue mutation.

T HE NINE SPECIES OF LOVEBIRDS ARE QUITE DISTINCT, even though some of them look similar. Some are very common in captivity, and some aren't suitable for captivity at all. A few species are very easy to come by, but most are very rare and not readily available for purchase. People who want to breed these rare love-birds often enter into a consortium to bring them from overseas, which takes considerable time and effort. This chapter takes a close look at each of the lovebird species, both in the wild and as pets.

Common Species

The following three species of lovebirds are those most com-monly found in captivity. They are the three you are likely to find in pet stores and are the most popular pet lovebirds.

The beautiful peach-faced lovebird is a popular pet. Peachies are also friendly and entertaining clowns.

Peach-Faced Lovebird (*Agapornis roseicollis*)

The most common lovebird in captivity today, the peach-faced lovebird represents the ideal lovebird to many beginners. Most peach-faced lovebirds are between six and seven inches long, and the relatively heavy build is reflected in a weight that may exceed two ounces, even in wild birds. Thousands of these lovebirds are bred each year for pet shop sales, and the species comes in perhaps more color variations (mutations) than any parrot except the budgie.

These are beautiful birds by any standard. In both sexes (which are not readily distinguished in this monomorphic species), the body is bright green and the lower rump and feathers above the tail are bright blue. The primaries of the wings are green with black toward the tips, and the tail has only traces of the black band found in most other species, along with some red and blue. However, the upper parts of the outer tail feathers often are bright red above and below. The entire face is reddish, with a broad bright red band running from the middle of the crown to the base of the beak and the top of the eye. The cheeks, throat, and upper chest are paler pinkish red (peachy), fading into the green of the belly. There is a very narrow white eye ring, the beak is yellowish white (horn colored), and the eyes are dark brown—nearly black—in adults. Peach-faced lovebirds are not in the eye-ring category, but their slight eye ring often categorizes them as intermediate. Juveniles have just a touch of pinkish red over the front of the face and the throat as well as black smudges on the beak, which disappear as the birds mature. They reach full coloration after the first molt—at about six to eight months.

This species prefers dry grasslands, shrubby savannas, and open woods. The birds can be found in a narrow strip of southwestern Africa extending from Angola through Namibia into Cape Province, South Africa. This species comes in an astounding number of natural color mutations (see chapter 9) that breeders capitalize on by using selective breeding, that is, by putting different colors together to create babies of specific colors.

As a companion, the peach-faced lovebird is a wonderful choice, friendly and feisty, cuddly and clownish. Hand-fed peachies are as loyal as dogs as long as you handle them frequently. However, be aware that when left alone too often or when in breeding condition, females can revert to unfriendly behavior and become a hazard to handle. Males are generally docile and will maintain their friendliness if hand-fed and handled while young. This species is highly unlikely to talk, with only a few individuals ever learning to say a word or two.

This yellow black-masked juvenile shows the distinct white ring that gives eye-ring love-birds their name.

The White Eye-Ring Lovebirds

FOUR OF THE SPECIES OF LOVEBIRDS ARE CLASSIFIED AS eye-ring lovebirds because of the characteristic fleshy white ring around the eye, called the periophthalmic ring. These birds are the masked, the black-cheeked, the Fischer's, and the Nyasa. They are all smaller than the peach-faced at about four and one-half to five inches. They nest in colonies and have slightly overlapping natural ranges. They will hybridize (when two disparate species mate and have offspring) in the wild if introduced into new territories and can produce fertile offspring.

Fischer's Lovebird (*Agapornis fischeri*)

The range of this eye-ring species includes areas just to the south of Lake Victoria, mostly in Tanzania, and perhaps including

This young blue Fischer's lovebird will make a wonderful companion and is a good choice for a first pet bird.

Burundi and Rwanda (where the bird may have been introduced), west of the range of the black-masked lovebird. There they were declining in numbers—possibly because of trapping for the pet market (local and international)—until recently, as a result of human intervention. These lovebirds have been introduced into cities in Tanzania and Kenya, and there they may interbreed with black-masked lovebirds, who also are introduced to that range.

The Fischer's is another truly beautiful little parrot, a little smaller than the peach-faced. The nominate birds have a green body with a yellowish green belly and a yellow to pinkish yellow breast that extends as a faint, broken band (a not-very-distinct yellow collar) onto the nape of the neck. The rump feathers are tinged with blue. The face is bright orange-red from the area above the beak to the throat and back to the eye and cheek (brighter above the beak), grading into brownish orange on the back of the head and the nape. Some birds appear to have the entire head pinkish red, especially when selectively bred in captivity. The beak is bright red in the normal and yellow birds, horn colored in the blue and white mutations.

The Fischer's lovebird is common in pet shops and occurs in a few stunning mutations, including lutino (yellow), blue (white, light blue, and black), and albino (white). Some mutations are difficult to distinguish from the mutations of the black-masked, so it's important to know what kind of bird you have before you begin breeding. Fischer's lovebirds breed readily and are good lovebirds for beginners (just behind the peach-faced). They are just as feisty as the peach-faced, perhaps even a little more so, especially the females. This species needs a lot of hands-on attention to remain tame.

It's easy to see how this black-masked lovebird got the name!

Black-Masked or Yellow-Collared Lovebird (*Agapornis personata*)

One of the most commonly bred eye-ring lovebirds, the black-masked lovebird—also known as the masked or the yellow-collared—comes from grasslands of Tanzania and southern Kenya and is abundant there; large populations now exist in cities of Kenya and Tanzania, outside the natural range. The nominate bird is dark green on the body and on the wings, yellow on the chest, and green on the belly and rump. The head, from the upper nape to the base of the red beak and down through the cheeks and throat, is blackish brown to black. The black face is sharply separated from the green back by a bright yellow band running around the nape to the breast, the yellow collar of the preferred European common name. In the very similar-looking black-cheeked lovebird, only the face and cheeks are black, and the back of the head and the nape are brownish; there is no distinct yellow collar, but there is a pale pinkish bib below the lower beak, and the black areas of the face are more brown than black. Black-masked lovebirds are bred in many color mutations, most popularly the blue, in which the green is replaced by blue and the yellow by bluish white.

As pets, hand-fed black-masked lovebirds are amiable and friendly, but parent-raised birds are skittish and shy. However raised, lovebirds who are handled frequently will remain the most tame. The black-masked are about as easy to breed as the Fischer's.

Rare Species

Because the remaining six species of lovebirds are rare in captivity, they are discussed only briefly below.

Madagascar or Grey-Headed Lovebird (*Agapornis canus*)

The only species of lovebird found on the island of Madagascar, the Madagascar lovebird is rare in captivity today. There is little breeding stock left from the days of open importation, so the species is rarely seen, even with hobbyists. This attractive little bird often is found in open woodlands, in dry grasslands, in fields, and near villages over all the island, except the central highlands.

This sexually dimorphic species is plain in color, lacking bright colors on the rump, tail, and wings, and has a small grayish-colored beak. Females are entirely green. In males, the head, nape, and upper breast is gray (bluish gray in birds from the very dry southern part of the island, sometimes recognized as the subspecies *ablectanea*). The rest of the body is dark green on the back and wings, lime green on the rump, and yellowish green on the belly. The female Abyssinian, or black-winged lovebird, is also uniformly green on the head but has a waxy red beak. The Madagascar has a thin blackish line across the tail feathers. The eyes of both juveniles and matures are dark brown at all ages. Juveniles look like duller versions of their sex, and they typically have black smudges at the base of the beak. This species is small, about five to six inches long. Wild adults weigh one ounce.

Black-Collared or Swinderen's Lovebird (*Agapornis swindernianus*)

This species has always been considered uncommon and has never become established in the fancy. It has a spotty distribution along the Atlantic coast countries of Liberia, Ivory Coast, and Ghana, separated by hundreds of miles from the major part of the range in a wide band across Cameroon and Gabon to Zaire.

Just over five inches long, these tiny lovebirds are an overall green with a black beak, black primary wing feathers, and a bright blue rump. The tail has touches of red on either side of the central feathers within the usual black band. The most prominent feature of the bird in adults is a conspicuous black collar around the nape of the neck that is bordered behind by yellow to reddish brown; the collar does not continue around the front of the neck. The sexes are similar in color, although the females are perhaps a bit duller. Birds from the eastern part of the range have a distinctly reddish brown color in the area behind the collar to above the wing, as compared with yellow in the western birds. The eastern birds are considered two distinct subspecies. Adults have a bright yellow iris. Immature birds are duller in color than adults, lack the black collar, and have dark eyes and a gray beak with black smudges.

Abyssinian or Black-Winged Lovebird (*Agapornis taranta*)

The Abyssinian lovebird has never been abundant in the fancy and is not considered easy to breed. This bird is a close relative of the red-faced lovebird but with a much smaller geographic range in northeastern Africa, entirely within the country of Ethiopia (formerly Abyssinia) near the Red Sea.

Abyssinian lovebirds are six to seven inches long and heavy-bodied, weighing more than two ounces. (Only some captive-bred peach-faced lovebirds are larger.) Adults are uniformly bright green, including the rump (most lovebirds have blue on the rump), with black primary wing feathers and an unusually broad black band around the tail. The belly is paler green than the back, with a yellowish tinge. Females have a solid green head; males have a broad red patch over the base of the beak extending back to about the level of the eye; the feathers around the eyes form a red ring. In both sexes, the beak is bright waxy red and the eye is dark. Juveniles look like females, but young males soon begin getting reddish feathers above the beak and may gain full coloration at about four months old.

Red-Faced Lovebird (*Agapornis pullarius*)

When they were kept more frequently in captivity, red-faced lovebirds were fairly easy to keep, but breeding proved difficult. They have rarely been bred in captivity. Red-faced lovebirds are common locally in central Africa, but they have a patchy distribution. They are uncommon to rare in western Africa (Guinea to Ghana) and more uniformly distributed in open lowland forests and grasslands from Togo to Uganda, Kenya, and Tanzania.

Dimorphic and Monomorphic

THREE OF THE LOVEBIRD SPECIES ARE DIMORPHIC, meaning there are visual differences between the sexes: Abyssinian lovebird, Madagascar lovebird, and red-faced lovebird. There are no visual differences between the sexes in the monomorphic species, so you either need to have DNA testing done on the birds or be a very experienced bird keeper to be able to tell the difference.

This six-inch lovebird is bright green with a bright blue patch on the upper rump. The tail has the usual black band, but it also has bright red on the feathers and may have bright yellow at the tips as well. The primary wing feathers are dull greenish black. Head coloration is striking: bright red from the crown over the entire front of the face down onto the throat. In females, the red is more of an orange or yellowish red than in males. There is a very narrow yellowish white partial eye ring. The beak is bright waxy red in both sexes, and the eyes are dark brown. Immature birds have grayish beaks, with the males showing a variable extent of reddish feathering above the beak and on the throat.

Black-Cheeked Lovebird (Agapornis nigrigenis)

For many years, these lovebirds were extensively trapped for the pet trade and are still found in South African markets and in Europe, although they are quite rare in the United States. The black-cheeked never was abundant, and today it is listed as endangered, with perhaps only ten thousand birds still living in the wild. Found almost exclusively today in Zambia in central

Africa, the total range of the species is the smallest of any lovebird, with many peripheral populations having become extinct within the last century.

This bird looks much like the black-masked lovebird but lacks the distinct yellow collar and has dusky brownish yellow at the nape and back of the head rather than black. The species also has a peachy-red bib over the breast that is not present in black-masked lovebirds. Unfortunately, these two species have at times been interbred, so the genes of the black-cheeked are present in many lines of black-masked lovebirds, resulting in some confusingly patterned birds. Additionally, black-cheeks can be found in several of the color mutations known for the black-masked, including the blue variety.

Nyasa or Lilian's Lovebird (*Agapornis lilianae*)

This species is found in only a few populations in southeastern Africa, from Mozambique to Zambia, Zimbabwe, and Malawi (which has a postage stamp with the bird's image). The bird remains common in the wild but is seldom seen in captivity. This is unfortunate, as the species is a pretty lovebird that looks much like the Fischer's but has a yellowish nape rather than the brownish orange of the Fischer's. The Nyasa also lacks the blue rump of the Fischer's and has a brighter red face. The general impression is of a Fischer's lovebird where the yellowish green colors of the upper back gradate into the colors of the head. Hybrids of both peach-faced and Fischer's lovebirds have in the past been offered as Nyasa lovebirds, but they have blue rumps, so don't be fooled. You can find Nyasa lovebirds in both lutino (yellow) and blue mutations.

This is a lutino lovebird of the orange-faced variety.

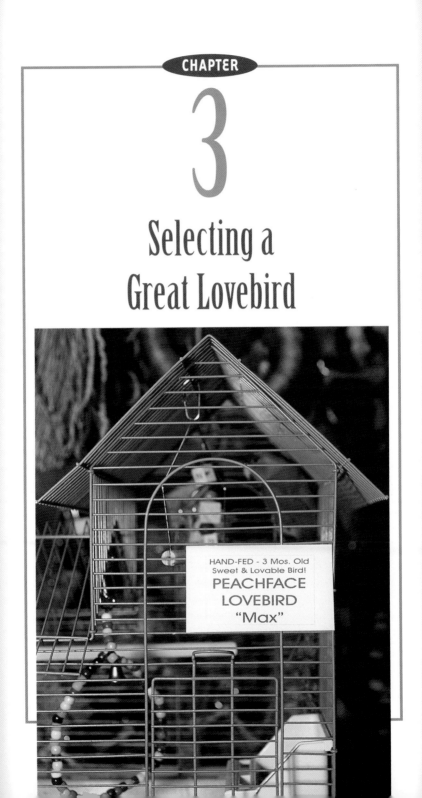

3

Selecting a Great Lovebird

HAND-FED - 3 Mos. Old
Sweet & Lovable Bird!
PEACHFACE
LOVEBIRD
"Max"

A blue black-masked lovebird has attracted a potential buyer's attention. Be sure that a bird will fit your lifestyle before you shop around for the perfect lovebird for you.

LOVEBIRDS ARE POPULAR PETS, AND IT'S EASY TO FIND A pet shop or local breeder who carries them, usually the three common species and their color mutations. Lovebirds are moderately priced parrots, much more expensive than budgies and often about the same price as cockatiels, but they are much less expensive than many larger parrots. Finding and buying a lovebird is easy when you do a little homework, but first you have to decide if you really want a lovebird and if the people around you will enjoy her as much as you will.

Is a Bird Right for You?

Having a lovebird or two (or more) is a joy. Their constant antics and chatter add liveliness to a household, and you won't get tired of watching them. They are beautiful and have their own distinct personalities, and when you put several pairs into a colony you get to watch an entire miniature avian soap opera play out every day. They are as dramatic as any television actor, quick to defend their beloved and their territory, and then a moment later turn to tenderly preen their mate. There are some downsides, such as noise and mess, but those actually aren't too severe with lovebirds.

There are, however, quite a few issues to consider before becoming the owner of a lovebird. Will your children or other pets get along with your new bird? Do you have someone to care for the bird when you travel? Do you have the space for the bird and all of her accessories? Some people consider having a bird as similar to having fish or small mammals. After all, they're both kept in a contained environment, unlike a cat or dog. Having a lovebird, a bird who likes to come out of her housing and interact with her human family, is actually very similar to having a dog. You may kennel a dog for part of the day, but you wouldn't dream of keeping her locked away all the time. The same is true for a lovebird. Before you get your bird, consider whether you have time for a dog. If you do, then this bird may be for you. However, many people keep lovebirds in pairs or small colonies, and they do very well together if they have enough space. In this case, your time will only be spent feeding, cleaning, and happily watching your birds interact.

The Cost

Are you prepared for the cost of owning a lovebird? Although most are not expensive parrots by today's standards, the housing and accessories can be costly. You could probably get a normal peach-faced lovebird for $25 from a breeder (about twice that from a pet shop), but you'll end up spending eight times that on

Lovebirds, such as this peach-faced, thrive on attention and need plenty of out-of-cage time to exercise and to interact with their human companions.

everything she needs to remain healthy and happy. Some of the rarer species, if you can find them, are quite pricey, and the newer mutations can run you $600—yes, for a lovebird! You also have to remember that someone took the time to hand-feed and raise your lovebird with love and care, and then the pet shop bought the bird from that breeder, and they have to make their cut, too. Not very many breeders are making a lot of money at their bird-breeding hobby or small business. It's a labor of love for most, so consider that in the price. The cost of the bird, however, is just the beginning. Consider the following basic costs:

- Cage: $75 to $300 or more
- Cage accessories (perches, toys, cups): $100 to $200
- Food: $15 to $30 a month or more
- Veterinary care: $150 to $400 a year

Time for a Bird

Do you have time to be a good bird owner? Lovebirds, like other parrots, need quite a bit of attention. A lovebird will languish and become crabby when neglected. She won't be as friendly as when you brought her home because she will quickly become unused to being handled. Lovebirds also need attention paid to their housing conditions, including cleaning, changing food and water, and making sure the cage is safe and free of drafts.

Can your schedule afford at least a couple of hours a day, ideally more, of attention for your new pet? Each bird deserves to be let out of her cage in a safe area each day and allowed to flex her wings and play with her favorite human friend. Most lovebirds are happy with some hands-on time and then are content to hang out on your shoulder as you go about your chores or watch television. They just like to be part of the action.

This pair of white-faced creamino pieds may bond more with each other than with a human and will help keep each other entertained.

Having a pair of lovebirds replaces handling from humans, but not if you want your lovebirds to remain tame. Tame lovebirds need to be handled daily. Some individual lovebirds can remain tame if you go on vacation for a week, but a pair won't—after just a couple of weeks, they will become so bonded to each other that they won't want much to do with a human companion. This isn't true in all cases, but it's true for most. Having a pair does cut down on the time factor, however, because you won't have to spend as much time entertaining your bird.

Do you have the time to keep a lovebird's cage clean? Like most birds, lovebirds are messy, throwing seeds around the cage and on the floor, trying to spill their water and bathing in it, shedding feathers, and, of course, pooping everywhere. Keeping a cage clean requires a schedule, ranging from spot-cleaning the perches each day to dismantling the cage once or twice a month. The tray below the grate needs to be changed daily, and the food

Allergies

LOVEBIRDS AND OTHER BIRDS SHED NOT ONLY FEATHERS but also feather dust and dander, which can be a source of respiratory problems for many children and adults. Dried fecal material also turns into fine dust that can cause lung irritation over time. Some sensitive people are subject to allergic alveolitis, a condition that occurs from breathing in all these contaminants, particularly those of budgies and pigeons. You can reduce these allergens with frequent bathing of your bird and frequent cleaning of the cage and the surrounding area, as well as investing in an air purification system. A doctor should examine a child who has a history of allergies before he or she is allowed to play with a lovebird or help in the bird's care.

and water dishes must be kept sparkling clean to avoid possible bacterial growth. A seed guard around the cage keeps most hulls and feathers off the floor, but some are sure to find their way to the ground. If you can't stand a mess, then you probably should reconsider having birds as pets. But most lovie fanciers will tell you that lovebirds are worth the trouble.

Children and Lovebirds

Children and birds do not always get along well together, but that is not a hard-and-fast rule. Small children often don't understand how to handle a bird, especially a small species, and can hurt or kill a bird just by holding her too tightly. Birds don't breathe the same way that people do, and holding them around the middle restricts their breathing. Children also react badly to even small nibbles from a bird's beak and could either let the bird

Here an older child is learning how to handle a black-masked lovebird. She may also learn to help take care of her pet, but she will need adult supervision.

escape or crush her while panicking. For such small birds, love-birds have a powerful bite that can draw blood, which is upsetting to both children and adults.

It is unlikely that a very young child can properly care for lovebirds. If your child badgers you for a lovebird, remember that maintenance of the bird will be wholly your responsibility. By the time children are twelve or so, some begin to develop a sense of responsibility and can take over some of the chores of bird care, although still under your supervision. In a few more years, the child may be heading for college, and then the chores again become your full responsibility.

Do You Have Other Pets?

Lovebirds are seldom compatible with other household pets. Obviously, a cat in the house may become a nuisance or a danger to the lovebird, wanting to treat the bird as a toy or as prey. The mouth and claws of a cat contain *Pasteurella* bacteria, which can lead quickly to serious infection and death from even a minor nip or scratch. Exotic pets such as ferrets and snakes offer similar threats. If you have any of these pets, keep them out of the bird room unless you are there to supervise.

Rats and mice are dangerous to birds as well; both will want to forage among the bird's droppings and will leave their own droppings, which can cause a bird to become ill. Keep fowl (poultry birds) away from parrots because they can pass along contagious diseases—this goes for raw poultry you're using for food as well.

Some dogs pose a dangerous threat to small birds, including sight hounds (bred to chase and kill small animals), terriers (bred to hunt and kill small animals), and some bird dogs. Other dogs may just be looking for a quick snack or something squeaky to play with, and what could be better than a lovebird for that? Some dogs, however, will just ignore the bird. You have to gauge the individual temperament of your own dog.

Lovebirds are very territorial and won't tolerate any other species of birds. They will kill small birds and will attack even the largest of birds; they have been known to gang up on larger birds as a team. Most lovebirds will get along fairly well with other lovebirds in certain situations, but they won't hesitate to attack and even kill each other if there's not enough space or they feel threatened. Females especially are known to kill other females (and interloping males); males are less likely to be this aggressive. Never put two lovebirds in a cage together and walk away unless you know they are a mated pair or you have observed them preening and kissing each other. If you have only seen them ignoring each other or showing signs of aggression, then putting them in a closed space together is like signing a death warrant for one of them, especially if they are two hens.

Noise and Legalities

Although they are small, lovebirds can be quite noisy. They can produce shrill chirping and other calls that carry good distances, certainly loud enough to disturb people in neighboring apartments or even closely spaced homes. The noise they make is mostly pleasant and probably won't bother the majority of people. But, if you live in an apartment or condo development, find out if you are legally allowed to keep birds. You won't be able to hide the fact that you have a lovebird.

Although any lovebird you are likely to find in a pet shop has been captive-bred from captive-bred parents, in some states

Lovebirds are little birds with big voices. This little blue black-masked lovebird is loudly screaming for attention.

and cities lovebirds are considered exotic pets, much as lions and giant pythons are. Check to make sure that owning a lovebird is not a violation of local ordinances. Surprisingly, it may be legal for a shop to sell you a bird but not legal for you to own it in a town just a few miles away. If you are trying to get the rarer lovebirds, you may have to fill out many forms and perhaps even pay fees or submit to an inspection of your premises if the bird is listed as a protected species. You also may have to pay extra fees if you have a bird shipped in from another state or even put the bird into a thirty-day quarantine if you move to or from another country. However, as of this writing, most states do not have any restrictions on owning or breeding lovebirds.

Choosing the Best Lovebird for You

Once you've decided that a lovebird suits your lifestyle (and that you will suit her needs as well), it's always best to visit your ideal bird before making a decision. It's tough to make a judgment about a bird's personality through an Internet photo or by just popping into a pet store and choosing the prettiest one. Try not to make an impulse buy. Work with breeders or reputable shops in your area to see if they have different birds available in the near future. Do your research before you bring the bird home.

Which Species?

Unless you are in a large city with many specialized bird shops, you will find that pet shops generally offer the three most common species of lovebirds: peach-faced lovebirds, black-masked lovebirds, and Fischer's lovebirds. Black-masks and Fischer's are similar in character, tending to be a little skittish,

Although they can be feisty and boisterous, peach-faced lovebirds such as this one make excellent pets.

fairly low-key, and needing quite a bit of hands-on time to remain tame. Peach-faced lovebirds are more outgoing and boisterous, but they make outstanding hands-on pets. Rarer and more expensive species are rare for a reason—they may be difficult to acclimate to cages, hard to breed, or just difficult to find in captivity—and therefore are considered birds for more advanced owners who breed them to help propagate the species. The rarer lovebirds also often do better in aviaries than in indoor cages.

Does Color Count?

THE MANY COLOR MUTATIONS OF PEACH-FACED, FISCHER'S, and black-masked lovebirds available in shops look very different from the wild-type birds (the nominate, or normal color), but these differences are only feather deep. The changes that affect feather colors don't change much else about the bird's behavior or personality. Just because a peach-faced lovebird is pied, yellow, or blue doesn't mean she is a different species. However, anecdotal evidence shows that some color mutations are less hardy than the nominate color. This may be a result of generations of inbreeding (also called line breeding). In the peach-faced and Fischer's, the green mutations (shades of green and yellow) tend to be very hardy, as are the pieds in the green family. The blue mutations in the peach-faced tend to be just a little less hardy.

Male or Female?

As a rule, male lovebirds are more easygoing and gentler than females. Females are more aggressive than males, and their bonds with humans more tenuous, or at least more mercurial; one day they are fiercely loyal and loving, and the next day they are just fierce. The main problem with hens occurs when they want to

As is true of many species, male and female peach-faced lovebirds are hard to tell apart. This pair will need a DNA test or an experienced bird keeper to distinguish them.

nest, which they will do whether a male is present or not. They will defend their nesting areas (even if it's the food bowl) and eggs.

There are some characteristic behaviors and physical traits that help to distinguish the sexes. Female peach-faced lovebirds tuck nesting material into the rump feathers to take it back to the nest. If you want to see which mature lovebirds in a group are female, give them a few strands of millet (including the long stem), a palm frond, or a piece of white card stock. The birds who descend on the material and begin tearing it into uniform strips and stuffing it into their rump feathers are female. The males do not exhibit this behavior. Female eye-ring lovebirds, however, carry around nesting material in their beaks and take it back to the nest. Males will carry material in the beak as well, but in general females are far more interested in it. Peach-faced females also are larger, stockier, and feistier in general. In Fischer's and masked, the females are a little stockier, but not by much.

In most mature lovebirds, you can feel the hip bones to determine gender; this doesn't always work, but it will about 75 percent of the time. Hold the bird gently and turn the bird upside-down; then put your index finger on the vent and feel for the hip bones. If they are very pointy and close together, you probably have a male. If they are blunter and wider, or if you can move them slightly by pressing very gently down with your finger, you probably have a female.

Overall, if you are an absolute beginner, look for a male love-bird rather than a female, but don't fret if you have to choose one from a cage full of birds without knowing the gender. The common lovebird species are difficult or impossible to sex correctly, so just choose the one you click with the most. Definitive sexing requires a DNA test of a blood or feather sample, which you can send in to a laboratory via the mail or have done at your veterinarian's office.

Hybrids

OCCASIONALLY, YOU MAY FIND A HYBRID FOR SALE, A *bird whose parents are from different species. The practice of blending two species is highly frowned upon by most avicultur-ists. Doing so weakens their bloodlines, and that's dangerous because there's no importation into the country anymore, and most breeders want to keep the lines pure for future genera-tions. Hybrids aren't bad birds, nor do they make poor pets—on the contrary, they can be very sweet and friendly. If you're adopting a bird and one of these hybrids needs a home, why not give it a nice place to live? If you're buying a bird, stick with breeders who are doing their best to preserve the species.*

These two masked lovebirds are already pals and would make a good pair to keep together as companions.

One or a Pair?

The old myth that lovebirds die when kept alone simply is not true. Tame single birds accept a human as a partner and devote their attention to him or her. However, if you have an untamed lovebird or one you aren't able to handle a lot, you should consider getting her a friend.

Try to buy a mated pair or a true pair. In this context, a pair means a male and a female who already know each other, have been living together, and get along. (Unless you want babies, keep them in close but separate cages.) If you just buy two birds out of a big cage, the birds could be two females or two males. If you get two females, you could have a problem with aggression; but if you get them very young, they should bond and be fine. Two males generally get along fine in the same situation.

Ideally, you want to buy two birds who have already bonded. Watch them in the pet shop or at the breeder's. If you see two birds sitting on a perch beside each other cuddling, preening, and kissing, it's likely that these two birds will be the same way when you get them home. In my experience, lovebirds either find love at first sight or they will never like each other. If you get two birds who are fighting, don't leave them alone together thinking they will eventually like each other. It's almost certain they won't.

Personality

The personality of your new bird is more important than species, sex, or coloration. Ideally, you will buy a tame, sweet, hand-fed youngster you can handle and cuddle from the start. Or, if you're getting a pair, your birds will be healthy and will have bonded. If you're adopting an older bird, she may come with some personality quirks, but that's no reason to pass her over. However, if you want a hands-on pet, and the lovebird you're considering bites and lunges, think twice about bringing this little lady home. She will be a handful to tame, and if you're not up for the challenge she may never come around. The bird you want is gregarious and curious enough to bounce over to look you in the face and possibly check out your hand, or even climb right up to your shoulder and make herself at home. Tame lovebirds are curious and will have to check everything out—your buttons, your pockets, your eyes, and your hair.

Hand-Reared or Parent-Raised?

Hand-raised, hand-fed, or hand-reared lovebirds have been taken from the nest as nestlings and fed by hand by an experienced breeder, usually starting at about two weeks of age or less; some-

Unless you want to spend a lot of time taming a bird, choose one who is already tame and easy to handle, such as this calm black-masked lovebird.

times they are reared right from the egg. A hand-fed lovebird comes to regard people as a source of food, play, affection, and conversation. Hand-rearing continues until the bird is completely weaned at about eight to ten weeks, and then she's able to go to a new home.

A hand-reared lovebird makes a great pet from the day you bring her home—that is, unless she hasn't gotten enough attention at the pet shop. Often, hand-fed lovebirds are sweet when they arrive at the shop but are fierce and nasty by the time they leave. Be aware that having a store employee hand-feed a baby lovebird might not be true hand-rearing, which is a process that's about more than just sustenance. A breeder has ideally handled the bird tenderly, given her a lot of attention and care, and weaned her slowly, not by restricting hand-feeding formula. (Note that not all breeders work this way.)

In contrast, some breeders allow the parents to raise and wean their young. These birds have had little experience with humans and won't be hand-tamed from the start. They tend to be shy, and it may take several weeks before a parent-raised bird becomes accustomed to being in a new home away from her parents and clutch mates. However, parent-raised birds who have had some socialization with humans can become tame with some patience (see chapter 6 for taming techniques). Often, parent-raised birds are a little hardier than hand-raised birds because they get the benefit of building a more natural immune system.

Sometimes, a lovebird has sat around in a pet store for so long, hanging out with other lovebirds and not being handled, that she reverts to fearful and skittish behavior. She will no longer want to be held and will bite and try to flee from being handled. Surprisingly, this bird is actually more difficult to tame than the parent-raised bird. This bird was once used to human hands and will be bolder in her attempts to flee or fight. This is not necessarily a bird to avoid, but you'll have to put in some extra effort to tame her.

Choosing a Healthy Bird

Now that you've decided on a species and perhaps a sex, you have to find a healthy bird. Only a battery of veterinary tests can tell you what health issues are happening with any particular bird, but even a novice to birds can look for the indications that

This is a healthy bird, with clean, bright eyes; a smooth and shiny symmetrical beak; and tight, smooth feathers.

a bird isn't feeling well. Avoid purchasing a bird out of pity because you think she might be ill, especially if you're new to birds. Make the healthiest choice possible following these guidelines:

Eyes: The eye ring should be clean, not badly wrinkled or covered with mucus or crust. The eyes should be clean and bright and alert.

Beak: The beak should be symmetrical and fit together naturally, not be scissored. Sometimes, a hand-feeder is too rushed and the beak grows oddly, with one side overlapping the other. A beak like this can be "trained" by a veterinarian over the course of a few months by filing it down to correct the deformity—don't attempt this on your own. The beak should also be clean and shiny, with no crusting on it, and it should be in proportion with the bird's head; an overgrown beak can be a sign of mites, malnutrition, or other disorders. The cere, which is the fleshy part just above the beak that contains the nostrils (which are hidden in lovebirds), should be clean and free of discharge from the nose.

Feathers: The body feathers should be smooth and tight. Twisted feathers can be a sign of disease. A broken feather is not a major problem and can happen in a crowded cage. Feathers should also be free of debris—a healthy bird tries her best to keep her feathers immaculate. Missing feathers in patches is either a sign of serious illness, self-mutilation, or cage mates picking on one another. Don't discount a bird who has lost feathers because another bird is picking on her—she's not a bad bird or a wimp, she's just in a cage with a bully. The people responsible for the birds should take care to separate birds who are aggressive toward others.

Feet and legs: Parrots have zygodactyl feet, with four toes arranged in an X, perfect for gripping and climbing. A young lovebird should have relatively smooth skin on the feet and legs, without large asymmetrical bumps, which can indicate a bacterial infection often found in birds kept in poor cage conditions. The toes should be straight, and all four nails should be present and of about the same length. Nails can be lost in cage wiring or bitten off by other aggressive birds, but they often regrow, so the absence of one or two nails (or more) is not considered a major problem. It's not unusual for lovebirds to be missing toes as well (having likely lost them to other lovebirds), and this does not

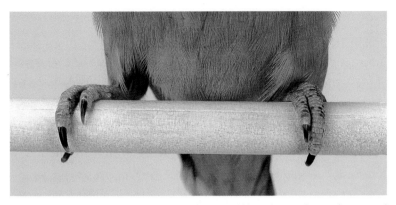

Be sure to check out the feet. They should be free of blemishes, with straight toes and healthy nails, as shown here.

adversely affect the bird. However, if you're looking at a young bird and she has several obvious foot problems, you should wonder about how she has been maintained and if she could have more serious problems that you can't easily see.

Attitude: The bird should have a bright and attentive stature. She should be playful, active, and curious. She should not be walking around with drooping wings or limping or hopping on one foot. She should not be sitting dejectedly in a corner, uninterested in the world, perhaps fluffed up and sleepy looking. Such birds often are sick and should not be purchased (and preferably not even touched). If you have reason to believe that any parrot in the shop is sick, don't buy a lovebird from that shop. Many parrot diseases are transmitted by contaminated food and droppings or through the air, so all the birds could be infected.

Where to Buy Your Lovebird

Some pet shops get a bad rap for not caring for their animals properly. The cages are filthy, the employees are disinterested, and the animals look the worse for wear. However, there are some stellar shops out there, both general pet shops and all-bird shops. In general, all-bird shops are great places to start, but even these are not created equal. You have to know what you're looking for to distinguish the good from the bad.

The health of the shop is as important as the health of the bird. This store is clean and well lit, with a range of supplies.

In a shop you want to avoid, there will be an unacceptable level of animal odor and usually poor lighting, and the shop will have a generally neglected look about it. A good shop will be well lit, and the birds will have decent housing and clean food and water. The staff will be friendly and knowledgeable, and if the employees don't know something about a bird, they will look it up in the paperwork. Prices may be higher here, but they're worth it, and you'll generally leave with a health guarantee, recommendations about veterinarians, and all the accessories you'll need for your new bird.

The size of the shop has little to do with whether it is good or bad. Little mom-and-pop shops can be immaculate, with staff members who understand a lot about the animals they sell. There are large mall shops with fancy cages and great lighting where birds with broken wings are on display, and with staff who can't tell a lovebird from a budgie. You can also ask the members of local bird clubs in your area, and you can be sure that they will have some very strong opinions on which pet shops to patronize and which to avoid.

Too Young to Leave Home

A WEANLING IS A BABY PARROT WHO HAS STARTED THE weaning process. She is fully feathered, can fly, and looks like an adult (with more muted coloring), but she is still dependent on her parents to feed her as she learns to eat on her own. This weaning step cannot be omitted in a captive-bred parrot. Weaning a bird is a long and sometimes frustrating process, and many pet shops don't want to do it.

Good shops will guarantee their birds are weaned, and selling unweaned birds is illegal in some states. Other shops may try to sell you an unweaned bird, saying that she will bond more to you if you feed her. It isn't true. The hand-feeder is often considered the parent, and birds are innately wired to leave the parents in search of a mate. Often, lovebirds raised and kept by the hand-feeder can become naughty and rebellious with them. Ask the shop if the bird is weaned, and watch her eat to make sure.

Unless you are experienced at hand-feeding, never buy an unweaned bird. This little violet chick is only about eight weeks old and is still being hand-fed.

The very large "big box" pet shops may not carry birds anymore, but they definitely carry bird supplies. Over the years, some of the big chains have stopped handling live birds because they proved too hard to maintain. The chains that still sell birds, however, often have well-trained employees who actually will take the time to look up details about individual birds for you; then again, you'll have to ask questions and judge for yourself.

Or, you can buy your bird directly from the breeder. You can find hobby breeders in the newspaper, through your local bird club, or online. These experienced people love their species and breed them for hobby or show. In some cases, they are concerned with producing babies of species that are becoming threatened in the wild. In other cases, they are breeding to create color mutations. Whatever the case, you're bound to find some breeders who are passionate about what they do. However, there

This is a mature white-faced violet lovebird.

At just three weeks old, this nearly featherless violet chick has about five more weeks until she feathers out fully.

are still quality issues to look for in a breeder. If you go to the breeder's home, look for clean cages and well-fed birds. It's not a good sign if the breeder seems disinterested with you or rushed with the babies. The breeder should not agree to sell an unweaned baby to anyone who has no experience with hand-feeding and weaning, although you may be allowed to visit your baby as she is being weaned. A good breeder will also have the name of the veterinarian he or she uses and will give you a health guarantee. Finally, a good breeder will offer to take the bird back (without a refund, of course) if you should be unable to care for her anymore.

Housing and Caring
for Your Lovebird

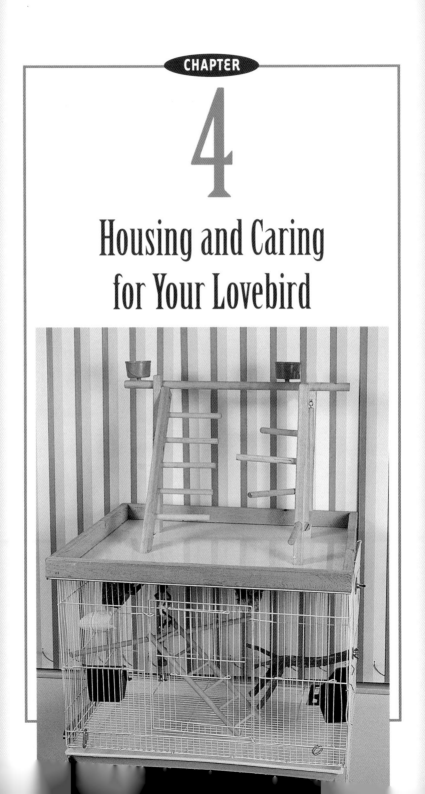

In addition to a large "home" cage, your new companion will need a travel cage or carrier, such as this one. Travel cages are invaluable for visits to the veterinarian for checkups or emergencies.

ONCE YOU'VE DECIDED TO BUY A LOVEBIRD, YOU HAVE TO buy the housing and accessories before you bring the bird home. It often takes a while to find the right cage in stock in your preferred color and size. You may have to look at several shops or search online before you find a suitable cage, and it could take you a day or more to get together all the basic equipment you need and properly set it up. If you buy your lovebird first and then start looking for housing, you might have a very disturbed little bird on your hands by the time you introduce him to his new home.

Choosing the Proper Housing

Cages can be expensive, and sometimes the temptation is to buy the most inexpensive cage first, intending to replace it later.

Unfortunately, inexpensive cages are often poorly built and last just a few years before falling apart and becoming dangerous. You will also have to invest in some quality accessories for your lovebird, which can be a lot of fun if you enjoy shopping. There are a large number of fun bird products on the market today.

Parrot Proofing

IF YOUR BIRD IS GOING TO SPEND ANY AMOUNT OF time outside the cage, you will need to parrot proof your home in case your bird is curious and wanders away. Here are some things to consider:

- Put away and hide all electric cords so that your bird can't chew on them.
- Remove all scented candles and plug-in air fresheners.
- Scrape off all flaking paint, especially on windowsills, and recoat with nontoxic paint (products used for a baby's nursery are fine).
- Make sure all windows have screens.
- Remove all lead from your home, including fishing weights, curtain weights, older or imported decorative pottery, and stained-glass windows and decorations.
- Eliminate anything with nonstick coating (pans, heating elements), and don't self-clean your oven.
- Remove any drowning hazards, such as full sinks and pots, close the toilet lid, and cover fish tanks and bowls.
- Put stickers on all windows and mirrors so that your bird doesn't think they're open spaces and try to fly through them.
- Move toxic plants so that your bird can't get to them.
- Remove all ceiling fans or place a piece of tape over the switch.
- Remove all halogen lamps or other hot lamps that your bird can fly into.

This trained black-masked lovebird is allowed to roam in a parrot-proofed room, but always under supervision.

How Big?

Lovebirds are active birds, and they demand spacious housing. The old rule for birdcages was that the bird should be able to spread his wings and turn around inside the cage, and if he could do that, it was sufficient. Well, today it's not enough to just be sufficient. We want our birds to have great lives, not just adequate lives. Updated research has shown that parrots need

Buying a Carrier

YOUR LOVEBIRD SHOULD HAVE A SAFE CARRIER IN CASE
you have to rush him to the vet or take him anywhere in the car.
It's not safe to put his cage into the car because the toys can fly
around and hurt him, and it's not sturdy enough in the case of an
accident. An inexpensive plastic critter keeper–type carrier is
fine, but you're better off with a molded plastic airline-
approved cage that you can strap into the seat belt. Don't ever
ride in the car with your lovebird on your shoulder. He can get
mischievous and distract you and—in the event of an accident—
he could easily get very hurt, lost, or even killed. Ideally, the
cage should have a door on the side and on the top, which will
make it much easier for the veterinarian to grasp him. Clear,
sturdy, molded carriers recently have become popular, and they
are nice because the bird can see you from all sides.

exercise to remain healthy, and a small cage doesn't provide for
that. It used to be thought that a bird with too large a cage
would have behavior problems and not remain tame. That is not
true. Some of the friendliest and tamest parrots live in large
aviaries. Ideally, the bird should be able to fly within the cage.
For most people, this is an unrealistic ideal. So just get the
largest cage you can for your budget and space, and if it's too
small, start saving for another one.

For small lovebirds, the minimum housing space should be
about 36" × 24" × 24". This is as small as you should go, and, of
course, buy a much larger cage if you can. Consider a walk-in
cage or an aviary. Remember that some large cages are meant for
small birds, like the lovebird, and some are meant for much
larger birds. You can distinguish between them by the width
between the bars. For the average lovebird, look for a width of no

more than half an inch. If the bar spacing is too wide, your bird might get his head stuck between the bars and panic, become injured, or escape.

Design

Choose a cage with a horizontal rectangular design. Birds move back and forth rather than up and down, so the vertical space is often wasted. A large square cage will do as well. Avoid circular cages because they offer the bird little security; parrots like to snuggle up in a corner of the cage.

Parrots also like to climb the sides of the cages, using the feet and beak to hang from the bars. Choose a cage with vertical and horizontal bars so the bird can adequately climb. Avoid cages with intricate scrollwork or bars that taper—these can catch a toe or trap the neck and cause serious injury.

Keeping a birdcage clean is challenging, so make sure the cage comes with a removable wire grate on the floor. The grate should fit over a tray that should easily slide out for cleaning. Ideally, the grate and tray will be made of the same durable material as the cage. Sometimes trays are made of plastic, which isn't as durable and will generally need replacing after a few years when it becomes brittle and cracks.

The cage bars should be thick enough for the bird to comfortably climb on them, and not so thin that the bird can bend them with his beak, as he might be able to do with an inexpensive cage. The bars should be punch-through construction, not welded—the welds can break eventually and ruin the cage, not to mention potentially injure the bird. Some people worry that cages with punch-through bars will rust more easily, but this isn't the case with quality cages. Make sure all the welds on the structure of the cage are solid and do not contain toxic metals or sharp edges (which they won't if the cage is from a reputable cage manufacturer). Beware of cheap imported cages that are attractive and large but are made from questionable materials.

The best cage material is stainless steel. These cages are more expensive, but quality stainless steel won't rust and will last the lifetime of your bird. Look for medical-grade or marine-grade stainless. Stainless is easy to clean because you don't have to worry about chipping paint, and you can scrape away debris without being particularly gentle. You'll know a cage is truly

This is a medium-size cage, with a large door, a stable base, and a removable bottom tray.

stainless steel if a magnet won't stick to it. Because stainless steel cages are very expensive, most people don't use them for their lovebirds, but they are worth researching if you like the look of stainless and money is not a concern.

Lovebirds are very often kept in powder-coated cages. Powder-coated cages are generally made of a lesser-grade steel, but they have a baked-on coat of paint; it is sprayed on as a powder and then melted onto the metal at high temperatures. Make sure that the cage company you choose has a reputation for quality, chip-resistant powder coating. Resist buying a cheaper cage with an inferior coating of paint—your bird can ingest the coating if it begins to flake, and this can be deadly. A good powder-coated cage should last more than ten years of you take good care of it.

Birdcages made from wood and acrylic are attractive (and expensive) but often don't offer adequate ventilation, which can cause illnesses in some birds, especially if moisture builds up in the cage. These are great for part-time living, but most of them should not be the bird's regular housing unless an adequate ventilation system is present or you take the time to thoroughly clean and dry the cage every day and give the bird adequate time away from the cage. Some acrylic cages have an open top or one side made from wire; these provide adequate ventilation.

As far as cage color goes, that's purely a matter of aesthetics. No color is superior to another. Dark-colored cages will show droppings more than lighter colors will. And speaking of droppings, try to find a cage that comes with a metal skirt that juts out from around the outside of the bottom of the cage, or one that has plastic or acrylic panels around the outside lower half of the cage. This will go a long way toward keeping the mess inside the cage.

The cage should be on its own sturdy base or stand or placed on a level and sturdy table. Don't suspend the cage from a hook or put it where it can easily be knocked over.

Some cages come in a dome-top style, some have a flat top, and some have a play area on top. Which one you choose is largely a matter of personal taste. Your bird will be fine with any of these choices. The playtop has an added bonus of giving your lovebird something to do when he's out of the cage, although most lovebirds won't stay for very long on a playtop. Make sure

Metal or plastic guards are preferred, but you may want to put a cloth seed guard around the bottom of the cage to keep food and feathers inside the cage and off your floor.

AS MENTIONED EARLIER, QUALITY CAGES HAVE NO TOXIC parts, but some inferior cages can have toxic coating, paints, and metals included in their construction. Zinc is the most prevalent heavy metal to avoid in your bird's housing and accessories. It is absolutely deadly, yet some birdcages and accessories are still made with it. Some caging materials—especially those from the hardware store that you might use to build your own cage—are galvanized, which means that they're treated with zinc to avoid rusting. Other items treated with zinc include wing nuts, chains, quick links, and nails.

that the playtop has a tray for easy cleaning, or it might be more trouble than it's worth. The dome top will give him a little more space. Some cages come with a top that allows you to easily add bird lighting, which is a nice feature.

Doors and Latches

The cage should have at least one large door and two or three smaller doors for feeding. Large doors make it easier for you to reach into the cage for cleaning. Doors must open smoothly and have good working latches and locks. For safety's sake, the door should swing out to open (like the door to a house) or fold down (like a drawbridge). Doors that slide up and down can slam down on your bird's neck like a guillotine if he tries to escape. Beware of doors that are made of plastic in a wire cage—these have been known to trap the necks of small birds.

Lovebirds can easily reach through a door and work a simple latch or lift up the door to escape. Eager lovebirds tend to slam the door up and down trying to escape, and the door can slam down on their necks. Lovebirds are adept escape artists. Get a cage that doesn't have these types of doors.

This is a cage setup with a sturdy base and bird-safe doors.

This pet shop offers new bird owners several options in bird cages, toys, and accessories.

Inside the Cage

The items that go inside the cage are also important, including perches, coop cups, and toys. Don't skimp on these items. Your lovebird needs quality accessories to remain content and healthy.

Perches

The cage you purchase will likely come with one or two simple perches, usually smooth wooden dowels made from pine or ridged perches made of plastic. These perches are fine, but they aren't adequate as the only perches in the cage. Equip the cage with several other perches of various sizes, diameters, and materials. Birds need perch variety in order to have healthy feet. Think of perches like shoes. If you wear the same shoes day after day for the rest of your life, your feet will probably ache and your gait may suffer. Try a variety of these various perches.

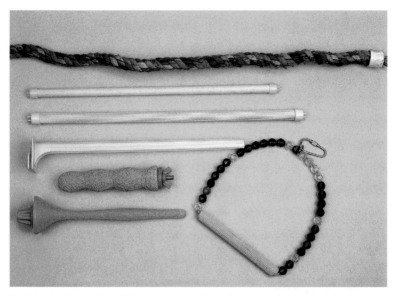

Perches come in a variety of sizes and materials, as shown here. Be sure to equip your love-bird's cage with a range of different types and sizes to keep your companion's feet healthy.

Natural wood: Manzanita, cholla wood, and other natural branches are great for a lovebird's feet. Some woods are very hard and will withstand chewing; softer woods will need to be replaced when they wear down.

Acrylic and plastic: Acrylic perches often come with toys attached and are virtually indestructible. Plastic perches are not the best—they can break easily and aren't as nice for the feet.

Concrete and sand: These so-called pedicure perches have a rough texture that helps to keep the nails trim. Your bird should have just one or two of these perches for variety, but they shouldn't be the bird's only choice. Birds often love these perches so much they become a favorite sleeping spot. Stay away from the sandpaper sheaths that are sold as perch covers. These can get moist and cause foot problems, and your lovebird may try to ingest some of the paper.

Rope: Rope perches come in a lot of fun, bendable shapes, but make sure the perch doesn't get frayed—trim all loose ends as the bird works on unraveling the rope.

Branches: Some branches from outdoor trees, such as birch, are good for perches, but don't use anything from outdoors if you think it might have been sprayed with pesticide, fungicide, or any other chemical. Scrub and dry all branches thoroughly before putting them in the cage. Some trees are toxic to pet birds, so check with your avian veterinarian.

Place the perches (at least four per cage) where they will not overhang the food and water cups to avoid contamination from feces. Don't place them over one another either, or feces will build up on the lower one. Remove perches once a week, and scrub them in warm soapy water. Allowing perches to become soiled can cause foot infections and other problems.

Tray Liner

For years, hobbyists have used newspaper to line trays of birdcages. It is inexpensive, clean, and easy to obtain. The newsprint also helps reduce bacterial growth. It used to be that the ink in newsprint was made with lead, but that is no longer the case. Today, the ink is nontoxic. Of course, newspaper doesn't look great, so some people prefer unprinted newspaper stock or brown craft paper.

You can also find all types of litters to put in the bird's cage, everything from shredded pine to ground walnut shells and dehydrated corncob, as well as recycled paper litter. If you want to use litter, choose one that absorbs moisture. This type is not easy for your bird to ingest, which can cause health problems, and it will not affect your bird's sensitive respiratory system. Ask your vet for advice. It's easy to see when newspaper is dirty and needs to be changed, but the litters hide debris. Litters also don't show fecal problems as well as newspaper does. You should also avoid the sandpaper sheets sold to place on the floor of the cage. In theory these help trim the nails, but in reality they harm the feet and can cause intestinal impactions if ingested.

Food and Water Cups

The ideal food and water cups are made of stainless steel. These are more expensive than plastic but are extremely safe, will last the life of your bird, can be boiled to make sure they stay clean, and don't add any chemical residues to the food (as some plastics may do). Cleaning plastic cups can cause very fine scratches to occur in them, and bacteria can grow in the crevasses. This can also happen with ceramic cups as they get older, but it won't happen with stainless. Some of the thicker plastic cups are okay to use with dry foods, but not for water or moist foods.

Using two sets of cups makes your daily cleaning a lot faster. This way you can just take out a dirty cup, replace it with a clean one, then wash and dry the used cup before the next change. You will need a cup for dry food, one for water, and another for moist foods. If you're getting two sets, that makes six cups total.

Place the water cup as far as possible from the food cup. Lovebirds like to dunk food into the water before eating, but it doesn't even matter that the food dish is far from the water dish—the bird will just carry the food over and make a nice soup with it. There's not a lot you can do to prevent this. The bird might also like to bathe and splash around in his water dish and might wet his food in the process. And keep all dishes above perches to avoid contamination from feces.

Sturdy plastic food cups are adequate for dry food, such as the seed and pellet mixes shown here. But stainless steel is best, especially for water and moist foods.

Replace water at least twice a day if your lovebird is a dunker. Some vets recommend using a water bottle or a sipper. It's true that the water inside the bottle gets much less contaminated than water in a bowl, but the bottle can also get clogged and prevent your bird from drinking. Furthermore, keep in mind that if you don't clean it well enough, bacteria can thrive inside the tube and near the ball bearing and cause illness. Besides, dunking food and bathing give a bored lovebird something to do—you'll just have to change it frequently.

Toys

Purchase a variety of types of toys so that your bird always has something interesting to play with. Switch toys on a regular basis, so there is always something new in the cage. Offer multiple toys at one time, but not so many that they turn the cage into a maze. Check toys weekly to make sure they have not become dangerous; ropes can unravel into strings that can wrap around a

Swings and chains such as these are fun toys for lovebirds, but be careful that nothing harmful can be chewed or pulled off and ingested.

bird's leg or neck; plastic edges may become sharp from chewing; climbing toys may become unstable. If a toy is falling apart, don't ditch it just yet. Keep it until you have several toys that need refurbishing, and then create one safe toy from all the usable parts. Some lovebirds are very hard on toys, although others can have the same toys for years without them showing too much wear.

When selecting toys, it is essential to keep safety in mind. Many curious lovebirds have been injured and even killed by playing with unsafe toys. Beware of small clappers in bells that can be removed and ingested, and avoid jingle bells altogether; the small slots are perfect for catching and breaking a toe. Again, check cotton rope toys often for fraying and long strands, or use sisal rope toys as a much safer alternative. Beware of toys that include spirals because they can pose a choking hazard, as can rings large enough for the bird to insert his head through. Steer clear of fabric-type huts, snugly toys, and plush toys. The bird can tear holes in the fabric and choke to death. This actually happens quite frequently, so only use these items with direct supervision or, better still, don't use them at all. Treat your bird's environment as you would that of a toddler. What looks like a potential choking hazard? What looks unsafe?

Inside the cage, hang up toys using only quick links, not key rings or spring clips, which can catch a beak or toe. Tighten quick links with a wrench so that your bird can't open them. The metal chain used to make a lot of bird toys can also catch a toe or foot and cause injury, so choose toys that are appropriately sized for your bird with chain links large enough for the toes to slip in and out of easily, but not so large that the chain can trap the beak. If a ring looks just big enough for the bird to put his head through, avoid that toy and find one with a larger ring. Try a variety of toys to see which ones your bird likes the best.

Wood: Wood is great for lovebirds because they love to chew. Most toys that are made from wood also incorporate other fun materials, such as rawhide (use unbleached only), pumice stone, leather, beads, and plastic shapes. Make sure that the wood is dyed using vegetable or all natural dyes and that the leather is vegetable tanned.

Acrylic: Acrylic toys are basically indestructible and come in a variety of designs. Look for acrylic play centers, similar to the type you'd offer to a toddler.

Plastic: Toys with plastic parts are fun for your bird, but remove them if he seems too voracious with them. A determined

Offer your lovebird a variety of safe toys, and change them frequently so your bird doesn't get bored. Always fasten the toys securely to the cage with quick links, as shown here.

lovebird can ingest bits of plastic and can become very ill or die if he can't pass them. Do not buy toys with very tiny beads or parts.

Rope: Cotton rope is commonly used in bird toys, but only use the type with very short strands, and use it with supervision. An eager lovebird can ingest rope, which can cause crop impaction, so keep an eye on how he plays with these toys. Sisal rope toys are safer.

Willow and grass balls, mats, and baskets: You can find these at most small animal supply places—they are nontoxic and are fun for birds to chew and play with.

Foot toys: These are toys such as rattles and dumbbells that don't hang on the cage but instead are scattered around the cage floor. Clean them often, and make sure to buy the appropriate size. Avoid foot toys that look if as a toe or head can get stuck in them.

Paper: More toys these days incorporate paper. Lovebirds—especially females—love to shred paper. Some toys come with spools of paper that are great fun for the bird to unravel. However, if your female lovebird insists on laying a lot of eggs (without a nest or mate), remove any paper products because these can stimulate her to breed.

Cage Cover

If your lovebird regularly wakes you up in the morning or if the area in which he lives is prone to drafts, you can use a cage cover to give him a little more rest and a comfortable night's sleep. Use a dark heavy material, such as a quilt or light canvas, preferably one made for your particular cage. If you use a material that's too flimsy, the bird can pull part of it into the cage and fray it or make a hole, which can pose a choking hazard.

Don't cover your bird in the daytime to make him quiet. If you have a sleeping toddler and you need to make a routine of covering the bird for an hour or so at the same time each day, that would be fine if the bird can come to expect it; but don't cover as a punishment or at random times for many hours. Your lovebird thrives on routine and won't understand why he's being shut away from his family.

Bird Lighting

Lovebirds have a gland at the base of the tail on the rump called the uropygial gland, or oil gland, which secretes oil that the bird gathers with the beak and spreads throughout the feathers. This oil contains the precursors to vitamin D that turn into the vitamin when sunlight hits it. The bird then ingests some of this oil during preening. If there's no sunlight to hit the feathers, there's a chance that your bird will develop a vitamin D deficiency. If you live in a place where your bird is unlikely to get sunlight, you'll have to invest in a full spectrum bird lamp or bird bulbs that mimic sunlight. These are easy to find in most pet shops or online. Merely keeping the cage near a window may not be sufficient.

Playgyms

Playgyms (also called playstands or play stations) are safe areas for your bird to play on when he's outside of the cage. There are many types you can buy, from PVC or metal to wooden or acrylic (or a combo of any of these). Choose one that best fits your budget and space requirements. The nicest stands have places to attach toys and give the bird something fun to do. Always supervise your bird when he's out of the cage.

The big problem with lovebirds and playgyms is that lovebirds rarely stay on them. After just a few minutes, your lovebird is going to flutter or fly off, looking for something else to do, usually something naughty, such as chewing the plants or power cords. Most really tame lovebirds will just fly (or run) to wherever you are. The finest place to stand, according to a tame lovebird, is on your shoulder or on your head. Lovebirds are more likely to stay on a very intricate wooden playgym that has a lot of toys, mirrors, and bells hanging on it. You can condition the lovebird to stay on the gym by placing him back there every time he flutters off and giving him attention when he's there, but not every individual is going to learn to stay put.

Cage Placement

As mentioned earlier, the cage should be placed on a stable, flat surface. Some cages come with legs as a part of their design, so

There isn't much on this playgym to keep these two masked lovebirds entertained. Embellish plain playgyms with toys and mirrors, or your bird will quickly become bored.

you'll just need to wheel the cage into place. Place the cage against a wall rather than out in the open. This will help make the lovebird feel more secure. A corner of a room is ideal. You can place the cage near a window but not right up against it, unless the cage is large enough for part of it to also be against the wall. Predators, cars, and people outside may disturb the bird. There should be access to natural light so the parrot can sense the passing of time and seasons, but a cage too near a window may become too hot or drafty. Drafty spots—such as those near an air-conditioner duct or heating duct or near a doorway to the outside that is constantly in use—should be avoided as well.

Your lovebird wants to be part of the family and should be within sight and hearing of his family whenever possible. A family room or TV room is an ideal site for his cage. Your bird likes hustle and bustle. However, don't put him in a high-traffic area, such as a hallway—he'll want people to stop and hang out in the room, not just see them as they pass by. A room that's quiet for much of the day, such as a child's room or a back room, also is not a good choice because the bird will become bored easily.

The kitchen is a dangerous place for birds. Many aerosol sprays, including room deodorizers and scented candles, can cause severe respiratory problems and even death. Birds are especially sensitive to fumes emitted from nonstick coatings on cookware and other heating elements, such as space heaters, popcorn poppers, and blow-dryers. If you have a bird, it is imperative to toss out all nonstick cookware. This sounds extreme, but the fumes from it have been shown to kill birds at regular cooking temperatures. The bird's respiratory system immediately fills with fluid, and the bird drops off the perch, dead. It's that fast. This means no nonstick grills, no self-cleaning ovens, and no nonstick pie tins and cookie pans. The kitchen also is home to such hazards as scalding water, knives, hot stovetops, and other dangerous equipment. The garage is a similarly bad place to house a bird because of the potential for toxic fumes and dangerous chemicals and equipment.

Cage Maintenance

Your lovebird's housing needs basic maintenance to keep it clean and safe. Here's a list of basic cage duties.

- Daily: Replace the newspaper in the tray every day. Check all toys for signs of wear. Clean food and water dishes.

- Weekly: Scrape dried feces with a wire brush or spackle knife, paying close attention to the bottom grate. Remove perches, scrub them in warm, soapy water, and dry them thoroughly before returning them to the cage. Rotate clean toys into the cage, and take the soiled toys out to clean them (but leave your bird's absolute favorites in the cage).

- Twice monthly: Take the cage apart or roll it outside and spray it down with a hose to remove feces and dried food. (If you can't take it outside, the bathtub will do.)

You will need to clean the entire cage thoroughly with soap and water at least twice a month. Be sure to rinse everything thoroughly.

Clean everything with warm, soapy water and rinse and dry well. You can disinfect cage parts, dishes, perches, and most toys with solution of 10 percent bleach and 90 percent water. Don't let bleach fumes near your bird, and make sure to rinse very well. Another great and very safe disinfectant is grapefruit seed extract (GSE), which you can find at any health food store. It is nontoxic, even in very high doses, and you only need between thirty and fifty drops per quart of water to kill most

Aviaries

AN AVIARY IS A SPACE WHERE BIRDS CAN FLY—THAT IS the single distinction between an aviary and a cage. Some cage manufacturers call their larger cages aviaries or flight cages even though they aren't very large. Certainly, a large cage is ideal for a lovebird, but if you want him to fly (which is great exercise and psychologically fulfilling for a bird), you will have to invest in something much larger. The smallest aviary for a lovebird should be 4' × 6' × 7', but larger is better.

Often, people keep aviaries outside in an area protected from the weather and predators. This is a great option if you live in a place with a warm climate or can regulate the temperature in the aviary. Lovebirds can be acclimated to cold weather if they're outside all year long and have safe, enclosed nests to retreat into when the weather gets rough. You'll have to cover the aviary with plastic when the weather is windy or snowy. Most lovebirds don't mind cooler weather, but most birds hate drafts and wind, so make sure the outside of the cage is protected.

Be aware that predators will come hunting for your birds and may either dig beneath the cage or pull the birds through the wire. The floor should be solid concrete or wire buried beneath soil or sand, and the sides of the cage should be double wired— like a cage within a cage—so that predators can't reach between the wires.

Clean branches and ropes are both good choices for aviary perches.

viruses, fungi, and bacteria. You can also put one drop in an eight-ounce cup of water to prevent organisms from growing in your bird's coop cup. The product is healthful for both topical and internal use, but make sure to dilute it for both.

5

Proper Feeding
of Lovebirds

Here are samples of pellets and seed mixes. Variety is important, but your lovebird will need more than seeds to be healthy.

FEEDING A LOVEBIRD ISN'T AS EASY AS OPENING A BAG of seed or pellets and tossing some into a dish. If you want your bird to be really healthy and avoid a lot of unnecessary veterinary bills, you have to get creative with your bird's diet. Lovebirds require variety in their diet, and they need nutritious foods in order to maintain respiratory health, feather quality, energy, and a happy spirit.

Your bird needs food all the time, so don't feel as if you have to take the bowl away unless you are cleaning it or refreshing the food. If you are feeding a variety of high-quality, nutritious foods, it is impossible to overfeed your bird. This chapter will explain a balanced diet to help you choose the best foods for your lovebird.

Your lovebird may enjoy nibbling on vegetables such as this broccoli floret. Offer small pieces in a water dish.

Vegetables

Vegetables are very important for your lovebird's diet. Wild lovebirds eat a wide variety of vegetable matter, so your lovebird is designed to digest and get the most nutrients from this type of food. Veggies are a great source of vitamins and minerals that your bird isn't going to get from seed or pellets. Lovebirds vary in how much enthusiasm they show for veggies, but most are hardy eaters, and you should be able to find a few healthy items that your bird likes. Dark green and dark orange veggies are the best for your bird because they contain vitamin A and calcium.

How you serve veggies is important for determining how much your lovebird will eat. Try veggies raw at first, chopped, grated, whole, and so on until you find something she likes. You can also cook veggies, puree them, and even juice them. In a pinch, frozen veggies will do, but don't use canned veggies because they contain too much salt. Many lovebirds will nibble and play with greens woven between the cage bars or put into a dish of water on the bottom of the cage. Don't use clips or wooden clothespins to attach the greens because these can injure the bird. Feed no fewer than four to five types of veggies a day.

Seed Moths and Fruit Flies

TWO TYPES OF BUGS PLAGUE BIRD OWNERS, BUT BOTH can be prevented or eliminated if you know how. Seed moths (or flour moths) feed on seed and grains, such as rice and flour. They come into your home with seed from the pet store. These little pests lay eggs in the seed and in your foodstuffs, and the pupae spin webs around themselves and then turn into little fluttering moths that invade your home. They are basically harmless, but they are incredibly annoying.

For starters, freeze all your seed for a few days after you bring it home. This is easy if you're buying less than ten pounds, but if you're buying very large bags of seed (twenty-five pounds or more), it's doubtful you'll be able to freeze it all. Put all seed—as well as all grain, rice, cereal, and other similar foods—into doubled-up plastic zipper bags, so the moths can't get at them. If you have an infestation, you can buy pheromone traps online or in any feed store, and you can vacuum up the rest.

The other pest you may have to deal with is the tiny fruit fly. These little bugs fly around in dizzying patterns, and they infest fruit that you offer to your bird. Once you have fruit flies in your home, they will multiply by the dozens, seemingly overnight. Start eliminating them by removing fruit from your bird's diet for a few days. Next, fill a long-necked bottle (such as a wine bottle) with about half an inch of wine or orange juice, and put it near where the bugs are swarming. They will fly inside the bottle and won't be able to get out. You can also try putting out a small dish of honey; they will get stuck in it when they go in for a feast. Don't use flypaper for either pest because you risk having your bird getting trapped in it.

Use organic produce if you can find it. Many types of produce have far too much pesticide, fungicide, and other chemicals on it, and washing doesn't do much to remove them.

Fruit

Although fruit is high in sugar, it is also rich in nutrients that your bird needs to thrive. Lovebirds will eat berries of all types—blueberries, raspberries, blackberries, strawberries, and others. They also eat tropical fruits such as mangoes, papayas, bananas, figs (fresh), and pineapples. In addition, they also like red apples and pears cut into wedges. Serve no less than three to four types of fruit every day.

A bird on a high fruit diet might have watery feces. She may also have feces that are odd in color because of additions to the diet, such as blueberries. It's important to remember that fruit rots quickly in warm weather and may attract fruit flies and various bacteria and fungi. Offer fruits in the morning meal, and

Fruits are an important part of you lovebird's diet. Be sure to offer a range of fruits, such as this dried sampling.

These pelleted foods are a good adjunct to your bird's diet, but they should not be the only source of nutrients for lovebirds.

then throw away the remnants when you get home from work. Don't mix fruits or veggies with seeds or other dry foods.

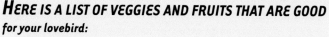

Veggies and Fruit

HERE IS A LIST OF VEGGIES AND FRUITS THAT ARE GOOD *for your lovebird:*

- *Bean and seed sprouts, beets, broccoli, brussels sprouts, cabbage, carrots, cauliflower, celery (leaves; stem chopped), corn (raw and on the cob), jalapeño peppers, kale, legumes and beans (cooked or sprouted only), peas, potato (cooked), red peppers, spinach, squash, string beans, sweet potatoes (cooked), zucchini*

- *Apples (remove seeds), apricots, bananas, berries (all kinds), cherries, citrus (every other day only), cranberries, figs, grapes, mangoes, melon (all types), nectarines, papayas, peaches, pears, pineapples, plums (remove pits from all fruit), pomegranates*

Pelleted Foods

More than a decade ago, manufacturers began producing processed foods designed for an array of parrots. These little pellets come in stars, crescents, disks, wheels, crumbles, and other shapes in many different sizes. Although pellets offer a solid base diet for all parrots, most bird keepers suggest that they should make up only part of the diet and should be offered along with a wide variety of cooked foods, seeds and nuts, veggies, and fruits.

Dietary Supplements

SUPPLEMENTING YOUR BIRD WITH VITAMINS AND minerals is a tricky business. For starters, most of the supplements found in pet shops aren't sufficient and will do little more than contaminate the water by allowing bacteria to thrive. Some supplements found online are better, but you can actually harm your bird if you overdose her. If you're feeding your bird right and she eats well, she shouldn't need supplements. If she has been ill, isn't eating well, is breeding and rearing young, or has been through a course of antibiotics, she may need some supplements.

You can find healthful supplements at the health food store, many of which are quite safe. Sprinkle greenfood and spirulina onto soft foods for some added vitamins. Do the same with nutritional yeast. Calcium powders can also be used similarly, but not every day. A pinch of powdered vitamin C in the water once a week can't hurt; try to find some emulsified vitamin A, and put it into the water a couple of times a week as well. It's important to rotate vitamins and minerals in and out of the diet so that the body can most effectively use them and so that you don't overdose. Of course, lovebirds will love to nibble on the old standards—the cuttlebone and the mineral block. Both add calcium to the diet. Just make sure to replace cuttlebones when they become whittled down.

The ingredients for the pellets came initially from research done on poultry, but ingredients have improved over the years. However, giving a parrot solely pellets has been shown to cause liver and kidney disease in cockatiels (and presumably it might do the same in lovebirds).

The key to feeding lovebirds correctly is to offer them the widest possible variety in their diet. This will include some pellets. Choose a brand that is organic and has no food coloring—if it smells fruity and looks like children's cereal, it probably has too many chemical additives. It's also important to choose a brand that your lovebird will actually eat. Some birds don't take to them immediately. It may take several weeks of patiently offering these foods before a lovebird tries them, and then at first she may only take one color or shape. Be persistent and be prepared to throw away a lot of food at this stage. Never try to starve a bird into eating processed foods or any other new foods. You can offer the new foods when she's hungriest, in the morning, and then offer her favorites in the early evening.

Commercially Prepared Cooked Foods

Cookable mixes are an exciting recent addition to the realm of parrot diets. These mixes contain a variety of human foods, including grains, precooked beans, pasta, and dehydrated fruit and veggies in a mix designed to be briefly microwaved or boiled, then cooled and offered to your bird. These cooked mixes are very healthful and can be used as a base diet for your lovebird, along with the fresh foods. Or you can be creative and make up the mixes yourself using canned beans (or soaked and cooked beans, never raw), whole wheat pasta, granola, nuts, dried fruits (sugar and sulfate free), and frozen veggies. Just cook up a batch and freeze it in portions that you can thaw each day. Remove the mixture from the cage after about eight hours—sooner in warmer weather.

Table Foods

Anecdotal evidence shows that the birds who live the longest are given people foods to eat, including fruits, veggies, and cooked foods as mentioned above, but also healthy foods you'd regularly eat. With just a few exceptions, your bird can eat everything you eat. When you're making your plate up for dinner, make a bowl for your bird too. Too spicy? Not to worry—your bird has far fewer taste buds than you do, and she can easily eat a hot pepper without flinching. Worried about cannibalism? Your bird isn't—share your chicken and turkey with her, but be sure that it's extra well done. Share your breakfast as well—birds love hard-boiled or scrambled eggs, but make sure that eggs are very well done because runny eggs may still contain bacteria from the chicken, and these can be passed on to your lovebird. Birds are not designed to digest dairy products, but a little cube of cheese once or twice a week can add some calcium to the diet, and most birds love it. Avoid milk, but you can offer plain yogurt. Soy products are great too—thawed frozen soybeans, soy milk (unsweetened) in a natural cereal, and soy cheese. Beef in small amounts is okay as well. Combined meals, such as lasagna, are great too (but no eggplant). A small piece of whole wheat bread makes a fun snack, as does air-popped popcorn. Because you probably don't eat the same thing every day, your bird won't fill up on anything that's too unhealthy, and the variety of table foods you offer will give her a lot of nutrients she wouldn't otherwise get.

Avoid feeding foods that are salty, and don't ever give junk foods loaded with salt or sugar. So no chips, salted pretzels, cake, candy, and so on. Chocolate is toxic for birds, as is caffeine, alcohol, raw beans, and avocados (so skip the guacamole). Don't feed raw onions or raw mushrooms either, but these things as part of a cooked meal are okay. It is also wise to avoid any

Toxic Foods

HERE ARE SOME FOODS TO AVOID:

- alcohol
- avocados—the area around the pit is toxic to birds
- caffeine
- canned dog or cat foods—contain bacteria harmful to birds
- celery, whole—serve chopped only because long fibers can become impacted in the crop
- chocolate
- dried beans
- eggplant
- fruit pits and seeds—all pits and seeds must be removed before serving, especially with apples, apricots, cherries, nectarines, peaches, plums
- junk foods—unsalted whole wheat crackers are okay
- pickled foods—too salty
- raw mushrooms
- raw onions—small amount of cooked onions in a meal are okay
- raw potato
- rhubarb
- salt
- spinach—serve sparingly; has vitamin A but binds calcium
- tomato—serve sparingly; never serve stem or leaves (tomato sauce in a meal is okay); never green or unripe

cured meats, such as bacon, sausage, and ham, because they are too salty and can contain unhealthy chemicals.

You can also make table foods specifically for your bird. Scramble some eggs (shell and all) with pellets, some dried spirulina powder, dried fruit, and anything else you have handy. You can make corn muffins using an easy mix from the store and adding healthful ingredients—peppers, pellets, nuts, soybeans, and so on. Freeze them in portions and thaw before serving.

Seeds

Seeds from the pet store are made primarily from grass and grain crops. Lovebirds in the wild do eat many types of seeds from trees, shrubs, and grasses. They have also learned to attack crops of grain, everything from corn to rice, and they are certainly adaptable enough to eat almost any seed or nut they can get into.

Seed is a perfectly fine food, but lovebirds fed on a strictly seed diet may eventually come down with serious health issues and may not live out a normal life span, which can be more than sixteen years if cared for properly. This is because seed is deficient in many of the vitamins and minerals that lovebirds need to survive. So you can offer seed, but not as the total diet. Give seed in the morning or in the afternoon, after your lovebird has had time to eat her other offerings. Leave some food in the cage at all times so she has something to nibble on if she needs a late evening or early morning snack. Depending on what else the bird is eating throughout the day, you can offer about a quarter cup of a good seed mix daily. If she's devouring healthier foods all day, she may not need as much. A seed mix designated for larger parrots should be fine. You can find mixes that include sunflower seeds and others that have safflower as the base. Sunflower seeds

This masked lovebird is munching on a seed mix. Offer seeds along with healthier fresh foods every day.

have gotten a bad rap because birds prefer them to just about anything else and will eat them to the exclusion of healthier foods. Sunflower seeds aren't bad, but they should be offered only after the bird has eaten healthier foods.

In addition to the common seeds such as sunflower, safflower, and millet, some more exotic things are offered in seed mixes, including almonds, pine nuts, pistachios, and even hemp seeds. Pumpkin seeds are excellent for lovebirds and are very healthy, as is buckwheat. As a rule, avoid mixes with cracked corn, a cheap additive of little nutritional value.

You can tell if seed is viable (able to produce life) and healthy for your bird by sprouting some on a paper towel. Take a teaspoonful of seeds, place them on a wet paper towel, and put the towel on the windowsill. Keep the paper wet and wait a few

The Grit Controversy

TRADITIONAL AVIAN LITERATURE ABOUT PARROTS (mostly European in origin) insists that parrots must be given grit to allow them to digest the seeds they eat. Only birds (such as chickens and pigeons) who ingest whole seeds, including the hulls, really need grit to help digest the seeds. Parrots crack the hulls and eat only the kernels. Grit is made by coarsely grinding oyster shells and similar calcium-rich materials, so the soluble type of grit also serves as a source of calcium, in theory. The insoluble type is made from quartz or silica (sand). Anecdotal evidence from both veterinarians and bird owners has shown that some birds may eat too much grit, which can cause crop impaction. Too much grit in the gut can also prevent the bird from properly digesting the food she eats.

days. If the seed is of good quality, most of it should sprout. You can sprout seed regularly using a cheap sprouting kit from the health food store to give your lovebird a very nutritious meal. Sprouted seeds and beans are among the best foods you can feed your bird.

Lovebirds adore millet spray, which is the millet still on the branch where it naturally grows. This is like candy to lovebirds, so offer it only about twice a week. It's also great as a reward during training and taming because it's pretty much irresistible to them.

When to Feed

Give fresh food first thing in the morning; this is when the lovebird is hungriest. Offer a healthy cooked grain, pasta, and bean mix; several fresh veggies and fruits; sprouts; and other table foods. Remove moist foods in the early evening, and offer more table foods and some organic pellets. Later in the evening, offer a quarter cup of a good seed mix.

If your bird likes to bathe in the water cup, why not offer a bird bath, such as this one?

Water

Lovebirds need access to fresh water all day. Change the water cups no less than twice a day. If you can, use only bottled or filtered water. Anecdotal evidence shows that birds who drink bottled water may live longer than those who drink tap water. Water should be at room temperature when you serve it. Expect your lovebird to occasionally bathe in the water cup and dunk food and toys in it—this is normal behavior. Keep the water as clean as possible. You can add one drop per eight ounces of grapefruit seed extract (GSE) to the water a few times a week to keep bacteria from growing in it. The days when you don't add GSE, you can add two drops of apple cider vinegar to the water dish. Both are very healthful.

CHAPTER

6

Training
Your Lovebird

This peach-faced lovebird has been trained to roll over on his back, which can come in handy during a veterinary exam.

As you might expect with a group such as lovebirds who vary in personality, not all members are equally trainable. They can't really be trained to perform complex behaviors; you'll be lucky if you can just keep your lovebirds from being too mischievous and getting into trouble. Lovebirds can be obsessive, and when they want something, they will try everything they can to get it. For example, if your lovebird wants to chew a particular plant, he will stop at nothing to get to it, and you'll never train him not to chew it—you'll just have to move the plant out of the room.

Lovebirds are also not great talkers, although one in a thousand (my very rough estimate) will learn a couple of words and phrases. However, it is not necessary to teach your lovebird to talk

Hand-reared lovebirds, such as this black-masked variety, are more likely to be friendly and trainable.

or do complicated behaviors. Lovebirds are lovely little birds with a lot to offer, but there are a few things you should teach your bird to keep him safe and to make him easier to examine at the veterinarian's office. This chapter gives you a short tutorial on lovebird behavior and offers protocols for taming and training.

Tame Versus Untamed Lovebirds

Your best chances for having a well-trained lovebird is to invest in a young bird (preferably about three months old) who has always been in close association with humans. Many breeders of lovebirds produce birds for a wholesale market and churn them out at as young an age as possible to cut down on overhead. Many of the birds are raised by their parents and then shipped to the market as soon as they are weaned.

Quiet Please

TRAIN DURING A QUIET TIME OF THE DAY WHEN THERE are few distractions for your bird. The room should be dimly lit (but not dark), and the TV and radio should be off. Sessions of about ten to fifteen minutes work well for most lovebirds, although some will become antsy more quickly. If the bird becomes excited or irritated, give him a few minutes to calm down, and then start over.

At the other extreme are breeders who specialize in hand-reared birds, as mentioned earlier. Here the young birds are taken from the parents and are fed by hand. They also are given lots of attention between feedings (feedings take place several times a day until weaning) and learn that humans are a source of food and fun. The young lovebirds bond with their humans and are friendly and affectionate.

If possible, look for a hand-reared lovebird of one of the common species. You can expect to pay more than for a parent-reared bird because of the extra time taken in his rearing, but the bird should be worth whatever you spend.

Lovebird Behavior

New lovebird owners are often baffled, dismayed, and thoroughly entertained by their lovebird's antics. Some of the behaviors that lovebirds exhibit are completely normal, although they may seem odd, whereas other behaviors are a result of illness or boredom. Before you panic about a new behavior or dismiss something unusual as normal, try to figure out what your bird is trying to tell you.

Normal Behaviors

Birds have very interesting body language that is quite obvious to other birds but isn't as intuitive to humans. There are dozens of behaviors that indicate mood and health. Here is a key for some of these behaviors.

Beak grinding: Before taking a nap or when getting ready for sleep at night, a healthy lovebird will grind his beak with a little gritch-gritch sound. This is completely normal and means that he's relaxed and sleepy.

Beaking: Some lovebirds can be very "beaky," meaning they will use the beak to communicate, which can often be mistaken for biting. Many lovebirds do this when they're young and will grow out of the habit if you do not make a fuss when it happens. Just put the bird down or walk away for a moment to discourage this behavior.

This blue mutation black-masked lovebird is just having a little stretch.

The blue mutation black-masked on the right is engaging in a little preening, while the green black-masked on the left appears ready for a nap!

Bowed head: This means, "Scratch my little head because it feels good!" Lovebirds particularly like it when you gently help them remove the sheaths over the pin feathers (new feathers) on the head and face. They also like being rubbed very gently on the eye and over the ear hole, although you have to have a very tame lovebird for him to allow this.

Crouching: If the bird is crouching with fluttering shoulders, moving his head slightly back and forth, this mean he wants to fly somewhere. If the bird is crouching with beak open, shoulders up, and nape feathers raised, he's saying, "I'm going to bite you if you come any closer!"

Flapping: If he's flapping while holding on to his perch, that's just birdy exercise.

Masturbation: A lonely bird will sometimes rub his vent on a favorite toy or even your hand. The tail is to the side and the bird is crouched over the object. Both males and females do this.

Nipping: A nip is a warning bite that isn't really intended to hurt; the bird is usually saying, "Back off a bit."

Preening: Birds preen to clean and order their feathers. When they preen one another, it's called allopreening.

Regurgitation: Parrots feed one another, usually males to females and females to offspring, to show affection and for sustenance. Some parrots try to feed their humans, but lovebirds rarely do that.

Shivering: If it's after a bath, the breast muscles shiver to create heat. Shivering, cowering, and screaming at the same time are a sign of a frightened bird.

Stretching: Birds stretch for the same reasons we do. When a bird stretches a wing and a leg at the same time, it's called mantling, and it looks a little bit like birdy yoga.

Tucking: Mature female peach-faced lovebirds will tear paper into uniform strips, tear up grasses or palm fronds and millet stems or anything else that seems like nesting material, and then stuff it into the feathers of their rumps and carry them back to the nest. Males do not do this, so if you see a lovebird performing this behavior, the bird is definitely female.

Yawning and sneezing: Bird yawn to clear their nasal passages and after preening. You can make a bird yawn by very gently massaging one finger over his ear hole. Birds also sneeze to clean their nasal passages. If you notice excessive sneezing and nasal discharge, however, take your bird to the veterinarian.

Vocalization

Lovebirds, like most parrots, vocalize the most in the morning at dawn and then again at dusk. This is completely normal, and there's not much you can do about it. Lovebirds can be noisy, and

This Fischer's lovebird is vocalizing—loudly. If your bird seems to be filling the void with his own noise, you may want to give him some background sound by turning on the TV or radio.

the more you have, the noisier they are. There may be quiet periods and naps, but for the most part these birds are persistent. Either get some earplugs or get used to it. Most bird owners don't hear the noise after a while and are surprised when other people entering the house mention it. Often, lovebirds will chirp sweetly and move the head during a daytime nap—completely asleep!

If your lovebird is chirping loudly for attention or because of boredom and is trying to get your attention, you'll have to reevaluate how much time you spend with him. Does he have a large enough cage? Does he have enough toys? Does he have plenty of food and water and the right kind of food? Is he healthy? Does he get enough attention and the right kind of attention? Is he happy in general? Would he be happier with another lovebird for a friend?

Birds don't like quiet because in the wild quiet means that there's a predator lurking about; so a bird in a quiet environment is either going to be louder or be silent because he's afraid to call attention to himself—a sad state indeed. Play the television or the radio on low for your bird during the day and early evening so that he feels safe. Turn it off at bedtime. Although lovebirds don't like other birds in their immediate environment, they do like birds in their periphery. Getting some finches, a canary, other lovebirds, budgies, or other small birds will keep your lovebird entertained and give him someone to talk to—just don't let them get together. Lovebirds also talk to wild birds outside.

Chewing

Lovebirds love to chew, and you're not going to be able to curb that behavior. The only thing you can do is to offer him safe items to chew on and supervise him when he's outside of the cage so that he doesn't chew on anything unsafe or valuable.

Biting

Lovebirds in the wild aren't known to bite. They threaten and they do fight, but more often than not, the bird on the receiving end of the open and threatening beak will just fly away rather than become injured. Birds have a complex body language and know when to stand their ground or move on. If you get bitten, it's because the bird is very threatened by you and has nowhere to go. A bite might also occur when you are invading the bird's territory, such as a hormonal couple's nest or cage area.

Biting can also be taught. If a bird bites you for whatever reason and you behave as if the sky is falling, the bird has learned

Some lovebirds communicate with their beaks, as shown here. Others use biting as a way to get what they want. Make sure you don't reinforce this behavior, but also don't push your bird to the point of frustration.

that a bite makes you react and makes you go away. That's exactly what the bird wants. In the wild, he'd threaten to bite, and the other bird (you) would fly away. Now he has just learned that the same thing works on humans. The idea is to not allow biting to work. Unfortunately, it does, so avoiding it is the only way to not reinforce the behavior. If you do get bitten, try not to have a huge reaction. Just turn your back and walk slowly into another room where you can make a fuss. Or, if you can, just stand your ground and squint at the bird, then tell him "no" in a lowered tone of voice, and try to pick him up again (if that's what you were trying to do when he bit you).

Some birds learn to bite to get their way. For example, if a bird really likes to be on your shoulder, he might bite when you reach your hand up to remove him and put him back in the cage. In this case, he's conditioned to think that your hand equals getting off of your shoulder to go back into the cage. All you have to do in a case like this is to give him treats and pet him while he's on your shoulder, and practice taking him off and then putting him back on, then taking him off and putting him onto a table, then picking him back up. Don't allow your bird to associate your hands with something negative, such as going back into the cage. He shouldn't think that every time you go to pick him up he's going right back inside. Instead, pick him up and take him somewhere else. Talk to him and pet him, then put him away.

In many cases, bites happen because expectations on the bird are too high or are unreasonable. Often, novice owners try to micromanage their birds' lives, which can result in very frustrated birds. If you are getting bitten, think about what you're asking of the bird and when you're asking it. Is it reasonable for the bird to not want to comply at times? Think of it from the bird's perspective. If every time you approach the cage you want to put him away, he might get the idea to hide from you or lunge as if to bite. He's no dummy! Of course, there are a lot of very compliant lovebirds who will do anything you ask, but if yours has a mind of his own, think of life from his point of view, and change your behavior to suit his. If you try it the other way around, you're only going to end up frustrated.

Feather Picking and Mutilation

Some parrots can become so bored or nervous that they begin to chew or pick their feathers. Although this doesn't happen very often with lovebirds, it's worth a mention here. Picking often starts as a nervous habit, like chewing your fingernails. Soon, the plucking becomes an entrenched habit and the bird removes his feathers faster than replacements can grow in, leading to a partially naked parrot who may even dig into his skin and produce bleeding wounds. Lovebirds aren't particularly prone to this behavior, but they are not immune to it either.

In some cases, picking isn't a result of a behavioral disorder but has a medical origin, as is the case in most picking lovebirds. Dry, itchy skin can cause it, as can respiratory illness, bacterial infection, or bodily injury. The first step to remedying picking is taking a trip to the veterinarian. In some severe cases, the veterinarian may suggest that the bird wear a collar to prevent him from further self-mutilation. This is a quick fix that can work, but you also have to find the cause of the problem to help the bird for the long term.

Hormonal Behavior

A female lovebird in breeding condition will show a change in personality. She may become cranky and possessive, may bite, and may vocalize more than usual. In general, mature lovebirds (those over about six months of age) will come into breeding condition in the spring, when the hours of light get longer. However, some lovebirds are in breeding condition all year long. You can prevent this condition by not allowing your lovebird more than twelve hours of light a day, no matter what time of year it is. If the bird is very hormonal, give her eleven hours of light and thirteen hours of darkness until her hormones stabilize. This doesn't work for all lovebirds, but it's the first place to start. Remove any nestlike objects that your bird likes to play with, such as boxes and huts, as well as any paper or anything resembling nesting material. These will stimulate the breeding condition and can cause territoriality.

If your single female lovebird does lay an egg (or more than one), you can allow her to have it for a few days, but then remove it from her cage; it will never hatch. If she lays more eggs, allow her to sit on them for longer until she becomes bored. Some birds will continue to lay eggs to replace the removed ones. If she insists on laying even more, try to figure out what's prompting her into breeding condition, and talk to your vet about her nutritional needs. Some hens are stimulated by the presence of nesting material, a dark corner, or something that resembles a nest box. Change the location of her cage, move around her toys and perches, and exchange her feed dishes for smaller ones to disturb the safety of her "nest."

When you remove her eggs, don't worry about her feeling upset. She will miss them for a little while, but soon she should be back to her old self again.

Positive Reinforcement Training

POSITIVE REINFORCEMENT TRAINING WORKS MORE *effectively than any other method. The idea is to reinforce anything you want your bird to do, using praise or treats, and to ignore the rest. If your bird is being noisy, ignore him, and then be quick to praise the moment he becomes quiet. Most of the time, all your bird wants from you is attention. Wild lovebirds are social creatures who are never alone, so your attention is the best treat your bird can get. When he's nice and quiet and playing on his own, walk over to the cage and praise him with a goofy, high-pitched voice and use his name. If the only time he gets attention is when he's misbehaving, he's going to learn that misbehaving gets the most attention.*

If your bird is hand-reared, he will already stand on your hand or perch on your finger, as this black-masked lovebird is doing. If not, you can train him yourself.

Cage Territoriality

Sometimes, lovebirds will become very possessive of their cages or other areas that they consider theirs (it happens mostly in females). Often this is seasonal behavior, but it can occur any time. You may find it difficult to feed the bird or clean the cage because she's attacking you. This is particularly dangerous with a hand-fed bird who isn't in the least bit afraid of humans. If the bird is fiercely protecting the cage and you can't even go inside to clean it, move the cage to another location or to another room, and change all the positions of the perches and toys. Change the bird's routine entirely for a while. This should be jarring enough to cause the behavior to cease. If you want to handle her, have her step up onto a stick and take her to another room for play-time. In extreme cases, you may have to remove her from the cage with a towel or bird net in order to handle her. This behavior should go away once breeding season is over in the fall, when the days shorten (although some lovebirds never really go out of breeding mode).

Hand Taming

Every lovebird, regardless of size and species, hand-reared or parent-reared, can be taught to stand on your hand. You can skip this step if your birds are going to live in an aviary and are able to fly and won't have any human contact; but if you plan to allow them out of the cage in your home, it's critical that you're able to pick up your birds without a fuss. A hand-fed youngster will probably already know how to perch on your hand by the time you bring him home. All you have to do to reinforce the behavior is to say "step up" every time the bird steps onto your hand and to make sure that your hand is always a stable, safe place to stand.

If you hesitate or are uncertain about the lovebird standing on your hand, the bird will come to view your hand as an unsafe place to stand and won't want to step up onto it. He may even bite if you insist. So begin all training with confidence. Have the bird step from hand to hand as you say "step up" and then "good bird!" as he does what you ask. Make sure to alternate the hand you carry the bird in, or he may want to stand only on the hand you use most often. In other words, if you always use your right hand to carry him, he may grow to mistrust the left. When you move to put your bird down, say "down" as he steps off of your hand onto a perch or the cage. Be consistent about giving these commands (cues) so that your lovebird learns what they mean.

Tame lovebirds can safely travel about on your shoulder—indoors only. This bird seems content to snuggle down into his owner's shoulder.

Most bird experts recommend that birds not ride around on your shoulder, but a tame lovebird is an exception. He can't do much harm if he bites (and if he does, you know not to put him there anymore), and he won't have any kind of dominance issues (which don't really exist anyway). To teach your bird to ride around on your shoulder and not flutter off, start by sitting still in one place and putting him there. Then gradually, over several days' time, get up and move around, first in the room where he lives, then in other rooms. Never take him outside on your shoulder or you risk losing him, even if his wing feathers are trimmed.

If your lovebird is a little skittish or is completely untamed, you will have to start more slowly. First, the bird's wing feathers should be trimmed to prevent flying, even if you want the bird to

Whittling Down

be able to fly eventually. (They will grow back.) It is impossible to hand-tame a bird who can fly—he'll just take off, and your training session will end with you trying to catch him.

Give your bird some time to adjust to his new home and family. Feed him through the cage bars, and talk to him soothingly, but don't stare at him—birds can find a direct stare threatening. It's a good sign when he'll take some millet spray from your hand or when he preens and stretches when you're nearby. This means that he's getting used to his new home and beginning to trust you. Start putting your hand inside the cage near the bird and then taking it out again. You are trying to desensitize the bird to your close presence. If you rush, you'll only succeed in scaring him. Once he gets used to being close to you, start by trying to touch him just for a moment, and then retreat. Don't scare him.

Next, remove a small perch from his cage (or get one that looks similar), and try to get him to step onto it. If he does, praise him and then let him step back onto another perch within the cage. Repeat this for a while; when he's comfortable, begin moving the perch toward the door. Take it slowly. When he seems ready, remove him from the cage. If he's scared, put him right back in. The idea is to make this fun for him and a pleasant experience. If it's negative in any way, he won't learn that being near you is fun or safe.

Once you can get him out of the cage, sit at an empty table or on the floor—someplace with few distractions and where the bird won't get hurt if he flutters away. You may have to eventually move to a smaller room where he can be easily retrieved if he flies. When he's comfortable, move your hand toward him, backing off if he seems afraid. Repeat this a few times a day until you can get your hand close enough to touch him. The idea is that you eventually will want him to step onto your hand, but you have to get him to trust your hand first. Offer him millet spray, and try to tickle his chest a little with one finger. When he's ready, put your

Always reward a good performance; it will reinforce the behavior. Most lovebirds appreciate a treat of a bit of millet spray.

finger lengthwise against his chest (like a perch) and push a little. This will set him off balance, and he will raise a foot to right himself. When he does, put your finger under his foot and lift. Ideally, he will step onto your hand.

Admittedly, some lovebirds aren't going to be tamed this way. They will need to be fished out of the cage with a towel and brought to a small room, such as the bathroom (toilet lid down, all hazards out of reach). Close the door, sit down on the floor with your knees bent, and plop the bird onto the top of one of your knees (wear jeans or thick pants to give him something to grasp). He's not going to be thrilled and may flutter away from you. Pick him up and start over. The idea is not to scare him but to have him see that, even though he's being handled, he's not being hurt and you are safe to be near. Speak to him soothingly and move slowly. After a few sessions of this, move your hand up your leg toward your knee and his feet. See if you can touch one foot for a moment, then retreat. Do this until you can touch his chest or even his beak. If he will tolerate it, have him step onto a perch and then back down onto your knee, and eventually you will work toward having him step onto your hand.

Never blow in the bird's face, squirt him with water, or flick his beak if you want him to trust you—these are some of the things that I have heard people try during training. Not a good idea. Just be patient and keep taming the bird gradually and gently.

Stick Training

Stick training helps to assure your bird's safety should he escape into a tree or perch high on the curtain rods. It's also helpful for the hormonal lovebird who's being particularly crabby or one who doesn't want to go back into the cage. Begin stick training by using a perch the bird is familiar with, and then move on to a long dowel, which you may have to place near the cage for several days to get your bird used to it. Repeat "step up" when the bird gets on the stick and "down" when you set him down. Ideally, your bird should learn to willingly step up onto a four-foot dowel, a broom handle, and a T-perch (a perch shaped like a T; the bird stands on the top part).

Talking

Most lovebirds won't learn to talk, but those who do are a constant delight to their owners. They are little wonders. You can't tell in the pet shop or at the breeder's which lovebird will talk,

This bird has learned to step from the cage to a perch. This training will make it easier to retrieve your bird if he flies up to a high "perch" in your house.

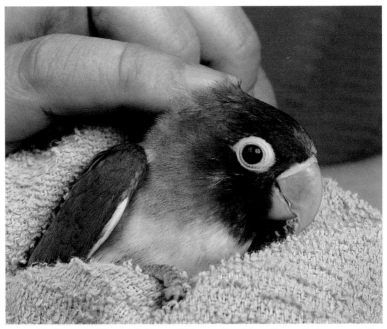

Here a black-masked lovebird shows off his towel training. If your bird accepts being wrapped in a towel, it will make veterinary exams and grooming tasks all the easier.

Towel Training

THERE WILL BE TIMES WHEN YOU OR YOUR VETERINARIAN will need to wrap your lovebird in a towel to be examined or groomed. Getting your lovebird used to the towel will help him from becoming stressed when he has to be restrained. Start with a smooth, soft washcloth, not one made from loose terry cloth that can catch a toe. Have the bird stand on the towel and offer him treats. Next, pull one of the corners up, and encourage the bird to take a few steps into the little tent you've made. After a few sessions and when he's comfortable with that, pull up another corner, then a third, until you can easily put one or more corners over the bird. Make it fun and don't rush it. Eventually, you should be able to drape the towel over your bird and have him think it's all in fun.

but anecdotal evidence shows that you can watch a group of cockatiels and choose the noisiest bird as the most likely to talk. This may work with lovebirds, but it hasn't been tested because no one chooses a lovebird for his talking ability

If you do want to try to get your lovebird to talk, remember that speech training is based on repetition. Tapes, CDs, and videos can influence speech, but it's doubtful that your bird will learn to speak from any of these mechanical tools. Whistling, however, is easy to teach from a recording.

Your lovebird may not learn to talk, but the key to training is repetition, repetition, repetition. This owner has her bird's attention—the first step in training.

7

Keeping Your
Lovebird Healthy

You owe it to your bird to keep her as healthy as possible. She will reward you with years of companionship.

LIKE OTHER PET ANIMALS, LOVEBIRDS CAN COME DOWN with ailments and have accidents, both of which require veterinary care from a trained avian veterinarian. Don't take your ill or injured bird to the pet shop hoping that the staff there will help you—they won't. If your bird needs a doctor, don't take her to a pet store for medical advice. Avian doctors are very specialized and are trained in the nuances of the many illnesses that plague birds, most of which present similar symptoms. It is a sad fact that most bird owners don't think to take their birds for routine check-ups. Unlike dogs and cats, most birds are good at hiding signs of illness until the condition is fairly advanced. Your avian veterinarian can detect a potential illness in your bird (perhaps a low-grade infection or a nutritional deficiency) and treat it early.

QUARANTINE IS A PERIOD OF TIME DURING WHICH A bird is kept away from other birds to make sure that she doesn't have any contagious diseases. Most bird owners find that thirty days of quarantine is sufficient for new birds. During this time, the bird should be kept in a totally separate facility, or as far from other birds as possible. Tend to your established birds first, change your clothes and wash your hands and arms, and then tend to the new bird. In general, once the bird's lab results come back clean, it's okay to move her into an area with your other birds.

Finding an Avian Veterinarian

Not every veterinary office has a vet who can satisfactorily work on birds. You may have to go outside your immediate area to look for a suitable vet. If you live in Florida or California, you're in luck—there are a number of well-qualified avian vets in those states. There are fewer board-certified avian veterinarians elsewhere—although they are around if you look—and an experienced avian vet doesn't necessarily need to be board-certified to be good. Start looking for an avian doctor as soon as you decide you will be purchasing a lovebird. Go to the Association of Avian Veterinarians' Web site at http://www.aav.org, and check out the public pages that list member veterinarians and hospitals. These are arranged by city and state and offer contact information. You can also ask a local bird breeder and members of a local bird club for the names of vets whom they use and trust.

In many cities and states, a pet shop is required to offer a limited guarantee on the health of the birds they sell. The guarantees can vary greatly, but most agree that the bird is healthy when

This veterinarian clearly enjoys interacting with birds. When choosing a doctor, be sure to look for an experienced avian veterinarian.

she leaves the shop and that if in a specific period of time (usually somewhere from three days to a month, seldom longer) the bird is shown to not be healthy (a hidden problem or appearance of a disease diagnosed by an avian veterinarian), the shop will replace the bird or perhaps return some or all of your money. Realize, however, that it's not the shop's fault if you do something to the bird to cause her to become ill. It is your responsibility to have a newly purchased lovebird examined by a competent vet as soon as you purchase her. This activates the health guarantee and proves that a health issue came from the shop, not your home. In many cases, only certification by a veterinarian will ensure that the shop will correct a health problem. Schedule an examination within a day or two of getting the bird, and, of course, get a written copy of the health guarantee for your veterinarian's reference.

Before you choose a veterinarian, find out if the doctor's specialty is in birds. Find out what kinds of avian clients the doctor has, and ask for references of people with lovebirds (sometimes they can't give references, but some offices will). Find out how long an appointment will take. If they say ten minutes, find another place. A thorough examination and grooming of a bird can take more than forty minutes.

The First Examination

You've scheduled a post-purchase exam with a person you believe to be a competent vet. Now what? Observe the doctor carefully, and realize that there are no dumb questions; ask whatever you

Schedule an exam as soon as you've purchased your bird. The vet will be able to confirm her health and will establish a baseline against which to judge future tests.

need to know to be able to care for your bird properly. Beware of the veterinarian with a poor bedside manner who won't take the time to answer your questions. The doctor should ask you about the history of the bird and take a thorough inventory of everything you say.

When the doctor looks at your lovebird, he or she will start by observing her through the bars of the carrier. Then, he or she will ask you to remove the bird, or more likely he or she will remove the bird using a towel to restrain her. There will be a physical exam, and the doctor should ask you whether or not you would like a wing trim, nail trim, and a beak conditioning if the bird needs it. (Beak grooming isn't done regularly, only if the beak has excess layers of keratin or is overgrown a little. A very overgrown beak is a sign of illness or poor diet).

Once the physical exam is over, the veterinarian will weigh your bird. This is very important, so be wary of the doctor who doesn't take the time to do this. The doctor will compare the weight of the bird every time she comes in for a checkup. The vet will then perform tests that will need to go to outside laboratories for analysis, which can take a few days to a week. He or she will take a blood sample to test for anemia, thyroid and liver problems, viral and bacterial diseases, and nutritional deficiencies. You may also ask for a blood DNA sexing test if you want to know the sex of your bird. Basic blood composition and chemistry levels will be taken and recorded for comparison with future tests as your bird ages. The doctor will then take a fecal culture and perhaps a culture from the bird's mouth. These will show if the bird has a yeast problem, a bacterial infection, other fungi, or parasites. All of these tests are absolutely necessary and are worth the sometimes steep price.

Annual Visits

Every pet bird should have an annual veterinary visit. Ideally, you will schedule two visits, one every six months, but one yearly visit is the standard. Ask your veterinarian to run the battery of tests and to do a physical examination of the bird. This will run you between $250 and $400, depending on where you live and what tests the doctor runs, but it is an absolute necessity—don't skip it. With a small bird such as a lovebird, you can probably get out of the vet's office with a $150 bill if the bird is in good general health. Truthfully, hobbyists who have a lot of lovebirds don't do all of these tests all the time. But they know the signs of illness and injury, and they can help the birds themselves or take them to the vet when they see a problem. If you are a novice with birds, you'll want to keep up the annual visit.

Beyond annual visits, you may have to take your bird to the doctor if you notice signs of something wrong with your bird.

A messy vent such as this one should be examined by a veterinarian to determine whether the discharge is caused by diet or illness.

Go to the Veterinarian

IN ADDITION TO ANNUAL VISITS, YOU SHOULD GO TO THE veterinarian if you notice the following behavioral changes or physical problems.

BEHAVIORAL CHANGES:

- *appetite loss*
- *attitude change*
- *listlessness*
- *panting and tail bobbing*
- *screaming (constant and panicked)*
- *sleeping often in daytime (fluffy and on two feet)*
- *sleeping on cage floor (fluffed up)*

PHYSICAL PROBLEMS:

- *beak scabby or scaly*
- *bleeding*
- *cat scratch or dog bite*
- *discharge from nares or eyes*
- *eye swelling or injury*
- *feathers missing in patches; oil on feathers (can be deadly)*
- *feet scabby or swollen; lameness*
- *ingestion of a foreign body (something not food); ingestion of poison*
- *loss of consciousness*
- *severe change in feces (lasting more than a couple of days or passing whole seeds)*
- *sticky substance in mouth*
- *vomit that sticks to the feathers and beak (not to be confused with regurgitation as a sign of affection)*
- *wing or leg broken*

Common Illnesses

Most illnesses lovebirds get are the result of a compromised immune system stemming from poor nutrition. Lovebirds are also notorious carriers of some illnesses, such as polyomavirus. Illness can also result from exposure to a contagious disease. What follows is a list of potentially deadly diseases that can affect lovebirds. Your veterinarian should be aware of these diseases and will know when to suggest a test if a certain disease is prevalent in your area.

Polyomavirus

Widely called budgerigar fledgling disease, this viral disease is generally spread from the parents to their young, and lovebirds are notorious for carrying it. It also can be spread by sneezing and through feces. Infected birds, usually nestlings, develop hemorrhages under the skin, stop feeding, tremble while standing in place, and may die. Survivors carry the disease the rest of their lives, and they should not be bred or be allowed to associate with other parrots. Your veterinarian can detect polyomavirus disease through DNA tests. There is a vaccine available to prevent it.

Psittacine Beak and Feather Disease (PBFD)

This viral disease is most common in parrots from Africa and Asia, but it is occasionally seen in American parrots. The most obvious sign is an incomplete molt that tends to produce twisted feathers in the wings and tail, as well as thinning of the body feathers. The circovirus that causes it is transferred from older birds to nestlings, where it may cause death after a long period of failure to thrive. Sneezing and contaminated feces are the most common ways of circulating the disease, but parents may spread

Whenever you transport your bird to the veterinarian, make sure the travel cage is secured in the vehicle, as shown here.

it to their young through regurgitated food. If a parrot survives, she becomes a carrier. PBFD is best detected by a blood test.

This is one of the few parrot diseases that you might be able to bring home after merely entering a shop or a parrot expo where an undetected carrier is present. You can carry it in on the soles of your shoes, in your clothes, and in your hair. The disease is almost impossible to detect in carriers without proper DNA tests, and it may be much more common than suspected, covering a wide range of species. Any time you go to a pet shop or visit a show, you should decontaminate yourself by washing with soap and hot water, changing your clothes, and cleaning the soles of your shoes with alcohol or a bleach solution before entering the area where your bird lives.

PET BIRDS CAN CARRY ZOONOTIC DISEASES (DISEASES *that can be transferred to humans), but it doesn't happen very often; and if you get your lovebird from a reputable source and you get a veterinarian checkup for her, you're unlikely to catch anything from her. Some individuals with immune deficiencies, the elderly, and infants are more susceptible to catching bacter-ial or viral infections from birds. For your own piece of mind as well as your bird's safety, do not allow the bird to kiss you on the lips. The human mouth is much more contaminated than a parrot's mouth, so you're more likely to pass something on to your lovebird than she is to you.*

Psittacosis

Bacterial avian chlamydiosis, caused by *Chlamydophila psittaci*, was once a greatly feared disease because it could be transmitted to humans, producing a sometimes-deadly form of pneumonia known as parrot fever. Parrots carrying the bacteria appear healthy (although some may produce lime green droppings), so a blood test is necessary to detect the illness. Another approach to preventing spread of psittacosis to humans is to quarantine all newly arrived exotic birds for at least forty days so they can be observed for signs of the disease and be given a preventive treatment of doses of an antibiotic such as chlortetracycline, which kills the bacteria. Unfortunately, having psittacosis once does not prevent a parrot from getting the disease again if she associates with a sick bird.

When psittacosis moves to humans, it causes chills, fever, and a serious pneumonia. Before the advent of antibiotics, the disease could progress to death, and as many as fifty to one hundred cases each year once appeared in the United States.

Today, parrot fever is uncommon and is most likely contracted by breathing in dusty fecal droppings from pigeons in old buildings and even near park statues. It is easily treated with antibiotics and rarely becomes a serious condition anymore, although lung damage can occur if the disease progresses without treatment.

Newcastle's Disease

More correctly known as *avian pneumoencephalitis* or exotic Newcastle's disease, this viral disease often attacks flocks of poultry, such as chickens, turkeys, and ducks. The paramyxo-virus-1 is spread through the air. Initially, it causes the bird to

Don't mistake wet feathers for messy feathers (a sign of illness); this bird will dry.

lose control of her head and wings, so she may stand in place or fall to the ground with wings drooped and head held at an unusual angle. Within a few hours or days, serious diarrhea and dehydration occur, followed by complete paralysis. When Newcastle's is detected in a flock of poultry, the treatment is usually to kill and burn all the birds before they can transmit the disease to other flocks. Even if a bird recovers from Newcastle's, she can continue to spread the virus through her feces.

The major carriers of Newcastle's are contaminated pigeons and house sparrows who spread the disease through feces dropped on pens and aviaries. It is possible, although rare, for lovebirds kept outdoors to contact Newcastle's in this way. Newcastle's is a legally reportable disease and must be treated very seriously.

Pacheco's Disease

This viral disease probably originated in conures. When the disease is present (usually in Amazons and macaws), the bird may produce chrome-yellow droppings and experience diarrhea, tremors, and a cessation of feeding resulting in death. Although a vaccine is available to prevent the disease, it is too expensive to be used generally. Blood tests are the only sure way of diagnosing the disease and its carriers. Birds known to be carriers should not be allowed to mingle with other parrots.

Proventricular Dilatation Disease (PDD)

Proventricular dilatation disease also has been called macaw wasting disease and is not common in lovebirds, although it has been reported in them. It is a contagious disease that attacks the muscles and lining of the upper digestive system, making feeding difficult or impossible. Loss of muscle tone follows. PDD often

Egg Binding

EGGSHELLS TAKE A LOT OF CALCIUM TO PRODUCE, AND
sometimes a hen doesn't have enough calcium in her diet to build
shells for the eggs she's producing. An egg with an imperfect shell
cannot be pushed through the end of the oviduct and out of the
vent to the outside. Instead, it becomes trapped in the oviduct.
This is a serious condition known as egg binding, and it can kill
your bird. Egg-bound hens stop feeding, sit on the floor with
drooping wings, and can lose the use of their legs. If you suspect
egg binding, get your hen to the vet immediately. Surgery may be
needed to remove the egg, although sometimes injections of
calcium supplements and hormones will help her pass it.

If you can't get to the veterinarian immediately, you may help
the hen pass the egg by putting her in a hospital cage or warm
brooder. Use a ten-gallon fish tank with a heating pad under
one-half of it, and raise the temperature in the tank to 99
degrees Fahrenheit. Cover the tank with mesh and then halfway
with a towel. Line the tank with paper towels, and put very
shallow bowls of food and water inside (ill birds can drown in an
inch of water). Place a few drops of mineral oil into her vent, but
only if you can see the egg. Keep a close eye on her so that she
doesn't get too warm or go into shock. Keep her there as long as
twenty-four hours to see if she will pass the egg. If she doesn't,
take her to the vet.

attacks weanlings, who get the virus from their carrier parents;
they may die after a short period of painful suffering and starva-
tion. If they survive, they become carriers. Researchers believe
that it is a virus, although that's in question at the moment. The
disease is best detected by a blood test. Carriers still can be kept
as pets, but they should never be bred and should not be allowed
to associate with other parrots. They may require a diet of partially digested or easily digested foods and medication with a
COX-2 inhibitor to prevent muscle problems.

Grooming

Grooming a lovebird consists of wing trimming, nail trimming, and possibly trimming the beak if necessary. Beak trimming should only be done by a veterinarian. You can learn to trim the wings and nails yourself, but most people like to have a veterinarian or experienced hobbyist do it for them. You can injure your bird during a grooming session if you don't know what you're doing.

Wing Trimming

To prevent flying, the primary wing feathers (the flight feathers toward the end of the wing) are cut back to where the wing coverts start (the feathers that cover the body of the wing). The wing muscles and bones are not cut, just the feathers, which have about as much feeling in them as your hair and nails. If you pull a strand of hair out of your head, it will hurt; if you cut the hair, it will not.

This owner is trimming the primary feathers to prevent the bird from flying. (Note that the styptic powder is simply part of the grooming tools; it is used to stop bleeding in nails, not blood feathers.)

You do not have to trim your tame lovebird's wings if you are going to parrot proof your home and be sure to close all windows and doors when the bird is out of the cage. Flighted birds get more natural exercise, and they delight in being able to go where they want. They are also much safer from family pets as they can more easily make a quick getaway.

If you need to trim your bird, your veterinarian will show you how to correctly hold the bird and spread out the wing out so that you can trim the first seven to ten flight feathers. Using a pair of scissors with blunt or rounded tips, cut the feather where it meets the wing coverts, about halfway up. Do not leave the first two primaries intact (this used to be customary but isn't anymore). Trim both wings to prevent uneven flight and uncontrolled landings and injury, and trim the same number of feathers from both.

Birds molt each year, replacing old, worn feathers with new, complete ones. This happens to the primaries of the wing as well as the small body feathers (contour feathers). Feathers are replaced in fairly regular sequences (for instance, a central primary is replaced first, then one on either side of it, then the ones to each side of these), but the molt may occur over a period of several weeks and sometimes more than once a year. This means that you have to keep a close eye on trimmed wing feathers and keep them cut back as they are replaced. Be careful not to trim blood feathers, those new feathers that still have a blood supply. You can see the vein in the middle of the feather as well as the white sheath that protects the new feather as it grows.

If you do happen to cut a blood feather or your bird breaks one, pull it out with one gentle tug to prevent further bleeding or infection, using a pair of needle-nose pliers to get a good grip on the feather. If you're too squeamish to do it yourself, take the bird to the avian veterinarian right away. I have left about as many blood feathers in the wing as I have pulled out, and the bird always managed to stop bleeding and shed the feather after a few days. To stop bleeding quickly, put cornstarch or flour on the wound, but not styptic powder—that is only for bleeding nails.

Nail Trimming

If your lovebird's nails get too sharp for you to comfortably hold her, or if the nail is longer than a slight crescent (which can affect the bird's feet), you will have to trim the nails (or have your veterinarian do it). Use special scissors with short, blunt blades notched to hold the nail (much like cat claw trimmers). A nail has two parts—the quick, where there is a blood vessel, and the dead part of the nail at the end. You will cut off only the dead, pointed nail tip without nicking the blood vessel and

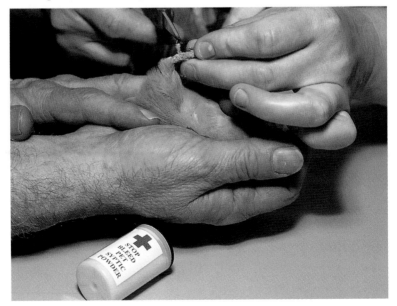

Two people are doing nail duty here; one to hold, and one to trim. Be sure to keep styptic powder (or cornstarch or flour) on hand to stop the bleeding if you inadvertently cut the quick.

causing pain and bleeding. If the nail is transparent, you can see the blood vessel, and the job is easy. If the nail is dark, trim only the very tip. Be sure to keep a jar of styptic powder (sold in most pet shops) or a dish of flour or cornstarch on hand; any of these can stop the bleeding.

If you don't want to traumatize your bird, you can use the sneak up method of nail trimming: Using very small clippers, such as ones for an infant, sneak up on one of your bird's nails while you're holding her or when she's on your shoulder. Quickly trim the very tip before she knows what you're doing. Do this for eight days in a row, and you will have trimmed all her nails with none of the drama.

Prevent Common Accidents

LOVEBIRDS ARE LITTLE AND CAN COME TO A TRAGIC END with one careless moment. Take steps to prevent these common household accidents:

- **Boiling or frying: Don't allow your lovebird anywhere near the kitchen when you're cooking.**
- **Drowning: Close all toilets, cover all fish tanks and bowls, and don't allow the bird in the kitchen unsupervised. A lovebird can easily drown in a glass of water as well. She will lean in for a drink or to bathe and then fall in and be unable to get out.**
- **Flying away: Please see that all doors and windows are closed when your bird is out of the cage, and make sure that no one is going to open them.**
- **Killed by another pet: This one is self-explanatory; keep all other pets away from your bird!**
- **Stepping on the bird: Always know where the bird is. The same warning applies to crunching it in the door or in the couch.**

8

The Basics of Breeding Lovebirds

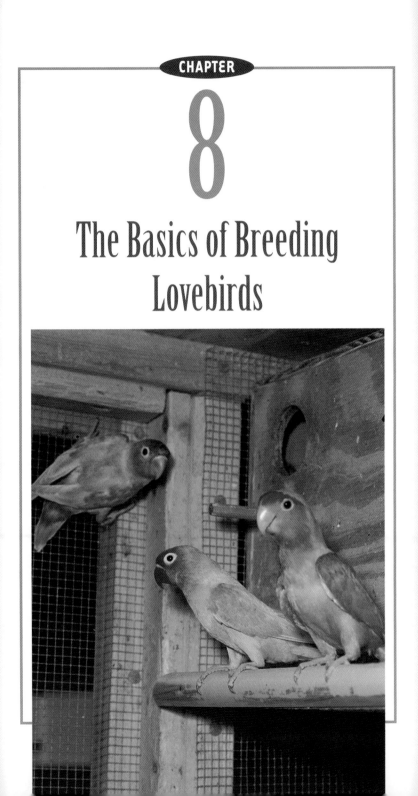

This black-masked lovebird and this blue-masked might look very different, but they are the same species and can be bred together—the babies will either be of the green or blue variety.

As SOMEONE WHO HAS BRED HUNDREDS OF LOVEBIRDS, I can tell you that it is an incredibly rewarding process but one that it is often fraught with tragedy and heartbreak. Breeding lovebirds is exciting and challenging, and in the end all you can hope for is healthy babies, a healthy breeding pair, and good homes where the babies will live long lives with a loving family. This is not a money-making venture for most hobby breeders. They do sell some of the babies, but the money they get usually will not even recoup the cost of keeping the birds and veterinary care. There's always one more unexpected expense, and the profits fly out the window. This chapter gives you the how-tos of basic breeding in case you're considering taking on this complicated venture.

Reasons for Breeding

Common lovebirds are relatively inexpensive, so you are not saving a great deal of money by breeding your own, especially when you consider potential medical problems and overhead. Unless you have exceptionally colored mutations and are quite familiar with lovebird genetics (discussed in the next chapter), you probably will not be able to improve your strain of lovebirds without a substantial amount of time and effort. But it can be done, once you learn how.

If you are just going to produce a clutch or two of babies (a group of babies from the same parents and the same group of eggs is called a clutch), you will be exempt from most regulations, but it never hurts to find out what the laws are in your area. Most states require that you put leg bands on your babies if you're going to sell them, and it's a good idea in any case. You can order bands from The African Love Bird Society, L & M Bird Leg Bands, Inc., or various other suppliers. More information about leg bands can be found at the end of this chapter.

One clutch probably will produce three to six babies, and you will not be able to leave the babies with their parents forever. They will need their own cages by the time they are about ten weeks old. If you're not going to keep the babies, you have to think about where to place them. Perhaps you can give a few babies to interested friends and guide them through the basics of getting started with lovebirds. You might want to keep one or two especially nice birds as personal companions to expand your existing family.

Breeding lovebirds to sell on a commercial level is a whole other issue. It's not easy to just put together a pair of lovebirds and then think you're going to sell the babies to local pet shops.

Bird Showing

MOST PEOPLE START OUT BREEDING LOVEBIRDS AS PART of the hobby, or fancy. For hobbyists, there are exhibition shows where you can exhibit your birds for awards and prizes, but mostly people show because it is fun and because they enjoy meeting other people who also fancy lovebirds. Shows are a great place to exchange information, learn a lot about color mutations, swap birds with other breeders, and perhaps even bring home a ribbon or trophy. Your local bird clubs will have more information on these shows, and most will likely hold a sanctioned show once or twice a year as well.

Commercial breeding is a very different process from breeding as a hobby. The key to successful commercial breeding is low overhead and guaranteed markets. A breeder must produce hundreds of lovebirds each year and be able to make a profit on selling them cheaply to wholesalers, who in turn pass them on to pet shops. It's quite an endeavor, and most people with even twenty pairs of lovebirds are still considered hobbyists. You also need permits to sell livestock and to transport them over state lines, health inspections, and tax forms. It's very involved.

So, for the purposes of this discussion, I'm going to assume that you're on your way toward breeding your first pair of peach-faced, Fischer's, or masked lovebirds as a hobby. The advice here is based on what I have done successfully with lovebirds and what my lovebird mentors had done before me. I'm sure that there are many other ways to successfully breed lovebirds, so it is best to do some investigation before you enter into a breeding program. It's a fun venture and not without its rewards, but don't enter into it lightly.

Age and Health

Most lovebird males can produce young when they are four to five months old, but most breeders recommend waiting until the bird is at least nine months to a year old. Remember: he not only has to be able to mate with the female, but he also has to be a good parent himself, and he'll be better at that when he's a little older. Females can produce young when they are about nine months old, but most breeders recommend waiting until she's eighteen months to two years old to give her a chance to completely mature. Laying eggs is hard on her body, and rearing young takes a lot out of both birds.

You also have to begin with a very healthy, hardy pair. They have to be in breeding condition, which means they've rested for a few months from breeding and have been fed a wholesome, hardy diet of healthy foods, especially those rich in calcium and protein. Ideally, they should be checked over by a veterinarian before you start to breed them. Parents can be carriers of diseases that they can spread to the young, even if the parents show no sign of illness.

Sexing

A major obstacle to breeding lovebirds is that the three common species are not sexually dimorphic—there are no visual differences between males and females. Females do tend to have a bit wider spacing between the hip bones to allow eggs to pass. If a bird lays eggs, it is certainly a female, but the absence of eggs does not guarantee it is a male.

The common lovebirds can be reliably sexed by using DNA tests of a blood or feather sample. Many laboratories specialize in these tests, and they advertise in bird magazines and on

If you plan to try your hand at breeding lovebirds, be sure to start with healthy birds who are in breeding condition, such as this pair.

the Internet. Today, the technique has become so common that DNA tests may cost only $25 each and results take less than a week. You can get materials for a DNA test directly from a laboratory or through your veterinarian, who also will provide the blood sample. Generally, the test kit contains a small piece of treated paper on which you place a few drops of blood. The blood may be obtained by trimming a nail back to the quick so that it bleeds for a few seconds before you stop the bleeding with styptic powder. Some laboratories even will do DNA testing from a few feathers pulled from the bird, since living feathers contain small amounts of blood at their base. (If you have a lot of birds and you don't want to go through the time and expense of DNA testing, see chapter 3 for tips on watching your lovebirds' behaviors to determine their sex.)

BE AWARE THAT A PAIR OF LOVEBIRDS SOLD IN A SHOP AS a mated pair may not be a true pair—they may be just compatible males or females. You can buy sexed pairs of lovebirds, especially of the more uncommon color mutations, where a knowledgeable breeder can predict sex by how different mutations are distributed in a clutch, but expect to pay more for them.

The Breeding Process

You can't just take a male and a female lovebird (or what you think might be a male and a female), put them into a cage together, and expect there to be love at first sight. Female lovebirds can be very aggressive and territorial of their space, and they can easily kill an interloper. So introducing them is a delicate process.

Introduce the two birds gradually. Put them into two separate cages in neighboring spots where they can see each other. Ideally, neither will be the breeding cage where they will live together; these can be small, temporary cages. If you have to have one of the birds in the permanent cage, it should be the male. Keep the birds separated for a week, then move the cages together so the birds can reach each other through the wires. If one bird (usually the female) tries to bite the other, especially on his toes, the pair may not be compatible. If they start sitting next to each other in their cages and try to kiss and preen through the bars, then they like each other. Introduce the birds into the breeding cage and watch them closely. If they seem affectionate, preening and kissing, then you have a match, and you can feel safe leaving them alone together. If one won't let the other one on any of the perches, chases him from the feeding dish, or attacks him, remove one of the birds immediately. This is not a match, and they will not get along, no matter how hard you try. Sometimes, the birds are just tolerant of each other but aren't a match. They kind of hang out, but there's no passion. It's unlikely that you'll get babies out of this pair. If you do have a pair who bonds, they will remain bonded unless you separate them and put them with other mates they like—in that case, they will rebond with the new bird. There's a common myth that female lovebirds will mysteriously kill their mates for seemingly no reason. I have not seen it happen. Females will kill other females in their midst, and sometimes a colony of lovebirds will gang up on a weaker bird, but even that is uncommon.

The breeding cage doesn't have to be any larger than the cage normally used, preferably a minimum of 24" × 36" × 48". The female needs exercise in order to remain in breeding condition and pass eggs. If she's in a cramped space, she may become egg bound.

After a few days of letting the couple get used to one another, add a wooden nest box to the cage. A budgie box is too small for peach-faced, and a cockatiel box is too large. Get a square box—about ten inches should work—or something similar. (Fischer's and masked like a more rectangular or L-shaped box and don't do as well in a square box.) The box should have a round hole in the front and a place for you to stick a perch just beneath the hole. This perch is important, because the male will likely sleep there at night (or sometimes on top of the box if it's inside the cage).

The top of the back or the side of the box will be cut in half and be able to slide in and out so that you can check on the eggs and babies. If you're putting the nest box inside the cage,

Here is one example of a cage with a wooden nest box attached to the outside.

choose one with a side opening so that you can put the back of the box against the bars. If you're hanging the box on the outside of the cage, then either opening will do.

To hang the box on the outside, you will either have to buy a cage with a special breeding door or clip a small opening near the top of the cage, usually on one side. Be careful how and where you clip so there are no sharp edges. You may have to screw cup hooks into the front of the nest box in order to hang it, but some boxes come with hanging attachments. Some lovebirds figure out how to open the sliding part on the nest box, so tap a very small nail or push pin into the sliding part and one on the fixed part, and then put a small rubber band or twist-tie over the two nails to prevent the bird from opening the box.

For peach-faced, fill the box to the bottom of the entry hole with regular pine shavings (not cedar) from the pet store.

The birds will kick out some of the shavings and make a concave area where they'll build the nest. For Fischer's and masked, just add about two inches of pine to the box—these birds prefer making their own nests. For all three species, supply some nesting material, such as fresh palm fronds (any type of palm will do), hay (not alfalfa because it molds), and card-stock paper (unbleached or white, not colored). The fresh palm fronds are especially important because the eggs need humidity to develop, and the fresh fronds give off moisture. Once the hen has laid eggs, you will regularly see her taking a bath and then going into the nest with her moist body to give humidity to the eggs.

The addition of the breeding box should put the pair into the breeding mode very quickly. The female will immediately check out the nest box. The male may check it out, too, but the female will often shoo him out (not always, but in some cases). Once you offer them nesting materials, the peach-faced hen will build a nest; the male does little to help. For peachies, nest building may take a week or so of going in and out of the nest, kicking out pine shavings and adding a little bit of material. For Fischer's and masked, it may take a bit longer because they tend to build elaborate nests with at least two chambers, one for the eggs and one to use as a sleeping quarters.

Just before mating, the male displays to the female by whistling, fluttering his wings, walking up and down the perch in a little mating dance, and trying to feed her regurgitated food. Eventually, the female accepts the male, and mating takes place on a perch or the cage floor. The hen lowers her body and spreads her wings out, inviting the male to get onto her back. He mounts her and presses his vent against hers. Mating is quick, but if you watch your birds often, you will be able to catch them in the act.

Egg Laying and Incubation

A few days after mating, the female lays her first egg in the nest box and generally lays one egg, usually every other day, until the clutch is complete at about four to six eggs (sometimes more). She starts incubating the eggs in earnest (called sitting tight) after most or all of the eggs are laid. The female will sit on the eggs, gently turning them and arranging them, and will leave the nest only to defecate. The male gathers food and stays close to the nest box, feeding the female several times a day, although females in captivity will very often venture out to grab some food and get a little exercise. Sometimes, if a hen isn't in good condition, she will become egg bound, unable to pass poorly formed eggs. Please see the information in chapter 7 on egg binding.

The babies inside the eggs begin developing when the hen starts to sit tight. They begin to hatch at about twenty-three days in the order in which they were laid. So, if there are six fertile eggs that all hatch, the oldest baby can be at least ten days older than the youngest baby, putting the little one at a disadvantage (more on this later). But, we're counting our lovebirds before they're hatched. Are the eggs even fertile? If you don't want to wait to find out, you can candle the eggs. A candler is a long, flexible flashlight that pinpoints light into the egg so that you can see through the shell into the egg. I recommend the commercial candler, which you can purchase via the Internet. Try http://www.birds2grow.com/prod-eggcandler.html or http://www.strombergschickens.com/products/candlers.htm.

The inside of the egg will look clear or yellow when it is first laid, but after about three days of incubation, the embryo begins to form a disk on the inner surface of the egg and sends out blood vessels. The blood vessels are very easy to see with the

Once this peach-faced lutino has laid her eggs, she will leave the nest only to defecate or to get a quick bite to eat or bit of exercise. Her mate will take over as food supplier, feeding her often throughout the day.

candler. If you candle the eggs a few days after the hen begins sitting tight and they are fertile, you should be able to see these blood vessels and a dark spot. The blood vessels grow every day for about two weeks, when the egg gets dark because the baby is filling it up. As the baby grows, there will be an air sac on one side of the egg, and when he gets ready to hatch, the air sac will draw down and become larger.

Don't check on the eggs too often. If the parents were hand-fed, just take a quick peek every day or every other day. If they were parent-raised and haven't had a lot of human interaction, check only a couple of times a week, or you'll disturb them too much. In general, lovebirds won't abandon the eggs or young because you've touched them or are checking on them. They are pretty good parents for the most part, although there are exceptions. If your birds are very skittish, don't check on them too much when they have eggs.

When the egg gets ready to hatch, you will be able to see (with the candler) the baby kicking and moving around inside the egg. Amazingly, the egg will also be cheeping like mad! About eight to twelve hours after you notice these signs, the baby will hatch by pecking at the shell with his egg tooth, a small sharp point on the beak, which falls off soon after hatching. Sometimes the mother will gently help the baby from the shell, but for the most part the baby does it on his own. This is an important process; the baby needs to be able to hatch on his own to develop strong neck muscles. However, sometimes the baby does need help to get out of the sac that surrounds him inside the egg if his nest or the environment is too dry. If he can't get out, he will die. If you're a novice to breeding, it's doubtful that you'll be in time to help him. If you are a little more experienced with breeding, and you know what to expect and how to handle

Foster Parents

IF THE PARENTS ABANDON THE BABIES OR TOSS THEM out and you have several pairs breeding at the same time, you may be able to foster an orphan under another hen, but most of the time lovebirds don't like that; it takes an exceptional pair to be able to take on another couple's baby. It's more likely that foster parents will accept a baby that is of the same mutation as their own babies.

This three-week-old nestling is snuggling into the breeder's hand for a little warmth.

babies, you can very gently use a toothpick to tear open part of the sac and even a very small part of the egg. Don't be tempted to take a baby out of the shell unless it's very clear that he's not going to be able to remove himself after forty-eight hours.

Both the male and female feed the young, and the female spends most of her time in the nest to keep them warm. The male passes food to the female, who then passes it to the young. When the babies are young, it's important to feed the parents healthy, soft foods that they can give to the babies. Some good choices are whole wheat bread, well-done hard-boiled eggs, greens, millet spray, and oatmeal and other soft cereals.

In the three common lovebirds, the babies stay in the nest for about six weeks. The fledglings are fed by their parents for two to four weeks after they start venturing from the nest before they are totally adapted to taking adult foods. When they are about eight to ten weeks old, the mother won't want them in the nest anymore and may become aggressive toward them because she wants to lay a new clutch of eggs. This is the time to remove them and put them in their own cage. If you want her to have more babies, you can just let the pair nest again. Add some more pine to the current nest. It's a good idea to thoroughly clean the nest after two clutches. Don't allow the pair to have more than three clutches in a row. You should rest them for the hotter months of the year and give them time to regroup and put on some weight. When you want them to stop breeding, just take away the box.

Hand-Raising Babies

Lovebirds generally make good parents and have a high success rate in fledging and weaning their young. Some breeders, however, will remove (called pulling) babies from the nest when they are about two weeks old and then hand-feed them. These babies are then very friendly with humans and make great pets. Sometimes, lovebirds aren't good parents and will bury the eggs or kill the young, and the breeder will have no choice but to pull the eggs or babies and raise them by hand. You won't know whether you'll have to do this until you try to breed your love-birds once. Sometimes, a pair is so fertile that they can have eight to ten viable eggs that hatch. In this case, you will have to pull the first four to six babies in order for the younger ones to survive. There's a huge size difference between a sixteen-day-old baby and a one-day-old baby. If you leave all the chicks in the nest, only the first four or five will survive.

Hand-feeding and weaning baby birds should be done only by people experienced with the process. This is not to say that you can't become experienced with it eventually, but you can't learn how to do it from reading a book. You have to find someone who will show you how to do it and guide you in the process. This is why it's important to find a lovebird mentor to help you (or someone who breeds cockatiels, budgies, or other small birds). An experienced breeder, someone in the fancy, should be willing to show you the ropes.

Banding Babies

IT'S A GOOD IDEA TO KEEP RECORDS OF YOUR BABIES, so you'll have to put closed bands on their legs when they are just two or three days old. Each metal band has a separate number for each baby, the year it was born, and the state abbreviation. You may also add your aviary's initials.

Putting the band on the leg isn't difficult, but it can be tricky, so it's best to have someone who knows how to do it show you the correct method. First, you have to be sure that the parents are going to accept the babies back into the nest once the band is on, or you'll have to raise them yourself. You also run the risk of the mother bird becoming irritated with the band and chewing the baby's foot off to remove it.

If you do want to band your birds, first lube the bird's leg with some petroleum jelly or antibiotic ointment. Next, place the band on the first two toes of the baby and use a toothpick to manipulate it over the next two toes, until it's on the leg. Remember, once it's on, there's no getting it off. Make sure that the chick's belly is completely empty when you do this, or you risk pressing on the crop and causing the chick to regurgitate, which may choke him.

9

Lovebird Color
Mutations

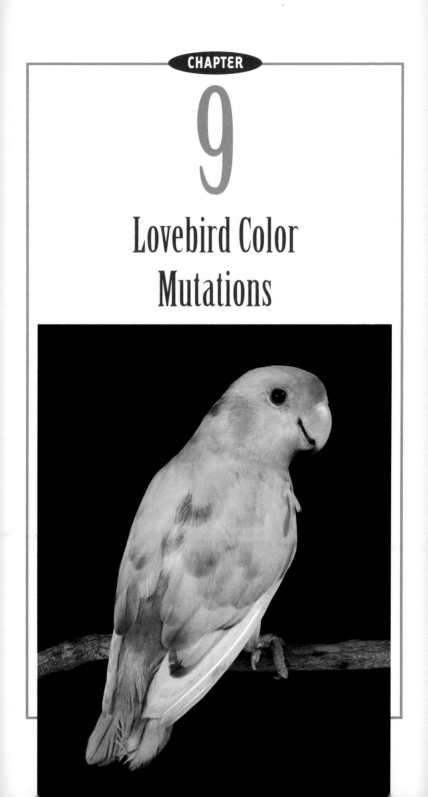

This is a group of fairly commonly found colors, one cinnamon (far right) peach-faced as well as normal, blue, and yellow mutation Fischer's lovebirds.

COLOR MUTATIONS IN THE LOVEBIRD ARE WILDLY popular, often more so than normals (the wild green color). There are thousands of color combinations possible in the peach-faced lovebird, and some of them are quite stunning. Some of the color mutations of Fischer's and black-masked lovebirds look so much alike, however, that the two species become very hard to distinguish.

This chapter simply serves as an introduction to how color mutations are produced in lovebirds and how you can learn to figure out what combinations of birds will produce certain colors in the offspring. This is not a comprehensive discussion, but it constitutes a short tutorial for genetic mutations in the peach-faced lovebird.

Color Mutations

Mutations are naturally occurring changes in the genetic structure of an organism's DNA. In the case of birds, this often shows itself as a change in color. These birds aren't considered mutants in the bad sense of the word, and there's nothing wrong with them. They just look different from the wild-type birds.

In the wild, most birds of a species are the same color. When a natural mutation occurs, the bird of a different color often doesn't live long enough to pass on her genes. Because she looks different from the others, she's an easy mark for predators. If she does reproduce, she may do so for only one or two generations, and then the genes she passes on may become overwhelmed by the more dominant genes in the wild birds.

In captivity, mutations are prized, and breeders do whatever they can to keep the genes of the mutations going. So when mutations show up in breeders' nest boxes, they know that if they keep breeding that bird, the genes will be passed on. Often, the breeder will breed parent to offspring and brother to sister (called line breeding) in order to concentrate the genes. This is a common practice, but it's not recommended as the norm.

So when you see a blue, yellow, or pied lovebird, that mutation just popped up somewhere in a breeder's nest box (and probably made the breeder faint on the spot). The breeder selected other birds to breed with that bird to best capitalize on the genes to get more birds of that color.

Simple Genetics

Genetics isn't really simple, but when you get the hang of it, you can predict fairly reliably what color offspring are going to occur with certain parents. Back in the old days before computers were

This is a young double-dark factor blue pied, also called a mauve.

popular, breeders had to do all the calculations themselves. Today, there are lovebird genetic calculators that do it for you. The one on the African Love Bird Society's Web page is great: http://www.africanlovebirdsociety.com/genetics/calculator.htm.

First, you have to know what's in the background of your lovebirds. For example, you can put two green birds together to breed and get yellow birds, blue birds, and just about anything else. This is because the male bird can be split to a mutation, meaning that he is carrying a gene for a recessive color or trait but does not show it visually. You can tell pretty well what's in the background of the parent birds by breeding them a few times. If they consistently have a certain color of babies, you'll know what is in their genes.

Here is an easy and very common example. Take a green male who doesn't have anything else but green in his background, and put him with a lutino (yellow) hen. Their babies will all be green, but their male babies will be split to lutino, meaning that they now carry the gene for lutino. The females can't be split to lutino without visually showing it (because it's a sex-linked mutation). If you put the green split to lutino male with a normal green hen, one quarter of the male offspring will be normal green, one quarter will be green split to lutino, one quarter of the female offspring will be lutino, and one quarter of the females will be normal green. As you can see, genetics is just a mathematical equation, and as you practice with breeding pairs you will get good at figuring out which pairs will give you the most interestingly colored babies.

The Green Series

The green lovebirds are the standard, the wild type, but there are mutations that stem off from the green that are still considered in the green series. The most popular is the lutino, a bright yellow bird with a red face. The eyes are also red because the bird lacks the melanin that the green has. In the green series are also the jade, the olive, and the green cinnamon, among others.

This lutino peach-faced lovebird is considered to be in the green series of color mutations.

This black-masked lovebird is obviously of the blue variety.

The Blue Series

The blue series birds look blue, but they aren't a true blue because the cells always have bit of yellow in them, although true blue mutations do occur in the eye-ring species. You will find some intermediate colored lovebirds (green or blue) called sea green and some bluer birds called Dutch blues. The lutino's blue cousin is the cremino, a very light butter-colored bird with red eyes, a whitish face, and a peach-colored brow. The albino, a white lovebird (which isn't really a true albino in the lovebird), is also in the blue series.

The Sex-Linked Mutations

The gene that makes the "ino" birds (such as lutino and cremino) is a sex-linked trait, meaning that it is carried on the sex chromosome and will show up visually in a female bird when no other dominant gene is there to suppress it and change her color (in the male, it behaves like the other mutations). The other sex-linked mutations are the American and Australian cinnamon, which have part—but not all—of the melanin pigment removed from their feathers; so they are a lighter color, and their flight feathers are light gray rather than black. The lacewing, a rare mutation, is also sex-linked. A new and stunning sex-linked mutation, the opaline, just appeared in 1997 and is a favorite of hobby breeders. This bird has a full hood of red (or orange or white) over the head, rather than having the color just stop at the brow.

One of the "ino" mutations, this creamino is in the blue series of mutations.

Dominant Factors

Some color or trait genes are dominant and will always win out over recessive genes unless both of the parents are carrying a recessive gene. The partial dominant genes are the single dark factor (which creates jades in the green series and cobalts in the blue and only has to be inherited from one parent), Danish violet, and American violet. The dominant genes are the double dark factor (which produces olives in the green and slates in the blue and has to be inherited from both parents), American pied, and green. The pied in particular, I have found, will affect most of the babies in the clutch if one of the parents is a visual pied. For example, even if babies from a pied parent are all green, they may have a wavy forehead line or different colored toes.

This is an example of a (young) pied lovebird of the green variety.

The pied in this bird is very subtle. He would be called either a mauve pied, a double-dark factor blue pied, or a pied medium blue, depending on who is naming the color.

Recessive Factors

Recessive factors have to be inherited from both parents: blue, whitefaced blue, seagreen, orange-faced, fallow, dilute (also called the golden cherry, cherry-head), and Australian recessive pied (a 90 to 95 percent creamy yellow bird with vague pied patches).

Longfeather

The longfeather mutation is the new kid on the block at the moment. This bird looks just like the normal peach-faced and comes in a few color mutations, but she is about twice the size of a regular peach-faced, with a very stocky body, thick legs, and a broad beak. She is also more vibrant in color than the regular peach-faced, and the red of the face and head extends much farther back onto the head than on the normal peachie. The mutation came out of Europe, but no one really knows where it came from, who bred it, or how they did it.

Appendix

Lovebird Societies

Here are some lovebird societies where you can go for information on the care and breeding of lovebirds.

THE AFRICAN LOVE BIRD SOCIETY
PO Box 142
San Marcos, CA 92069
http://www.africanlovebirdsociety.com

THE AFRICAN LOVEBIRD SOCIETY OF AUSTRALIA
PO Box 422
Pennant Hills, NSW 1715
http://www.nb.au.com/ALBS/

Other Online Sources

AMERICAN FEDERATION OF AVICULTURE
http://www.afabirds.org

ANIMAL NETWORK
http://www.animalnetwork.com

GOOD BIRD!
http://www.goodbird.com

PARROT PAGES
http://www.parrotpages.com

Glossary

allopreen: when birds preen one another

blood feathers: feathers that are just emerging from the skin that have a sheath and a blood supply

cere: area of skin above the beak that contains the nostrils (nares)

clutch: a group of babies from the same parents from the same group of eggs; also, the same group of eggs, as in a *clutch of eggs* or a *clutch of babies*

dimorphic: displaying visual physical differentiation between the sexes

DNA sexing: determining the sex of a bird by using a blood test

grit: coarsely ground oyster shells and similar calcium-rich materials (soluble); quartz or silica (insoluble); used to aid digestion, but not necessary for most lovebirds

GSE: grapefruit seed extract; used as a disinfectant and as a healthful supplement in drinking water

hand-feed: to pull a chick from the nest and rear it by hand

hookbill: name often given to parrots because of the shape of the beak

hybrid: offspring resulting from the successful mating of two different species

molt: the gradual process of shedding and replacing the feathers

monomorphic: displaying no visible physical differentiation between the sexes

mutations: in the lovebird natural color variations

nares: the nostrils

periophthalmic ring: the distinct naked ring around the eye

preen: to groom the feathers with the beak

Psittacidae: the parrot family

psittacosis: a zoonotic disease also known as parrot fever; a treatable bacterial infection that rarely occurs in parrots today

quarantine: a period of time during which a new bird is kept away from other birds, usually forty days

self-mutilation: feather picking, or plucking, often a sign of illness or psychological distress

species: group of individuals or populations sharing a common appearance and evolutionary history and capable of interbreeding with each other to produce similar offspring

split to: a male bird carrying a color gene he is not visually showing

subspecies: a group within a species sharing a feature of appearance that differs from other subspecies of the species and is found within just a portion of the range of the species

uropygial gland: the oil gland at the base of the tail (on the rump) that aids lovebirds in weatherproofing their feathers

wean: the process whereby baby birds learn to eat on their own

zoonotic diseases: animal diseases that are also transmittable to humans

zygodactyl: having a foot pattern that forms an X, with two toes in front and two in back

Index

lovebirds (*Agapornis*): about, 9–13, 17–19, 35–36; choosing your, 44–49, 51–54, 102–103, 124–125; common, 21–28; other pets and, 41–42, 139; rare, 28–30
lovebird societies, 142, 159, 167
lutino color mutation, 32, 160–161, 163

M

Madagascar lovebird (*Agapornis canus*), 11, 12, 14, 15, 28–29, 31
maintenance. *See* cleaning and maintenance
male lovebirds, 47, 144. *See also* sexing lovebirds
mantling (stretching), 106
masturbation, 105
mated pairs, 48, 146. *See also* breeding
medical tests, 127, 128
millet sprays, 98
mineral blocks, 92
molt, 130, 137
monomorphic, 23, 31, 45. *See also* sexing lovebirds
mutations. *See* color mutations

N

nail trimming, 138–139
nest box cage attachment, 147–148
nest building: communal nesting, 16, 25; as female trait, 46–47, 106; materials for, 148–149; preventing, 49, 111–112
nestlings, 153, 154–155
Newcastle's disease, 133–134
newspaper as tray liner, 73–74, 83
nipping behavior, 106
noise considerations, 42, 106–108
Nyasa lovebird (*Agapornis lilianae*), 12, 32

O

online resources, 167
opaline color mutation, 163
organic vegetables, 90

P

Pacheco's disease, 134
palm fronds, 149

parent-raised lovebirds, 49–51, 114–118, 151–152
parrot fever, 132–133
parrot proofing your home, 62
peach-faced lovebird (*Agapornis roseicollis*), 149; about, 12, 17, 23; feral flocks in Arizona and Florida, 15; longfeather mutation, 165; monomorphic nature of, 23, 31, 46, 47; nesting behavior, 46, 148–149; personality of, 22, 23–24, 44, 45
pedicure perches, 72
pelleted foods, 92–93
personalities: cage design and, 65; dynamics of, 36; escape artistry, 69–70; of healthy birds, 54; importance of, 49; need for family membership, 82; in pet shops, 50–51. *See also* behaviors; specific species
pet shops, 50–51, 54–57, 124–125, 146
pets other than lovebirds, 41–42, 139
pied color mutation, 164, 165
placement of cage, 80–82
plants, toxic, 62
playgyms, 70, 80, 81
playtop cage design, 68–69
polyomavirus, 130
positive reinforcement, 112, 114
powder-coated cages, 67
preening, 79–80, 106
prepared cooked foods, 93–94
proventricular dilatation disease (PDD), 134–135
psittacine beak and feather disease (PBFD), 130–131
psittacosis, 132–133

Q

quarantine, 124
quick links for toys, 77, 78

R

rare species, 28–30, 45
recessive genes, 165
red-faced lovebirds (*Agapornis pullarius*), 12, 16, 30, 31
regurgitation, 106